BUCKSKIN,
BULLETS,
~AND~
BEANS

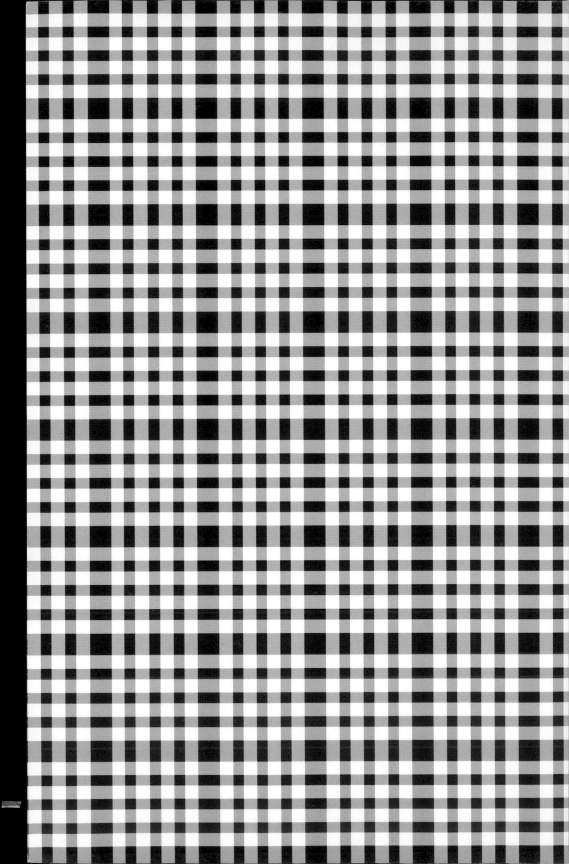

BUCKSKIN, BULLETS, AND BEANS

*Good Eats and Good Reads
from the Western Writers of America*

EDITED BY
BOB WISEMAN

PHOTOGRAPHS BY
CHRISTOPHER MARCHETTI

NORTHLAND PUBLISHING

The publisher wishes to thank the following companies and individuals for generously contributing their beautiful wares and collectibles to the pages of this book: Tableware and accessories courtesy of Dillard's Department Stores; Golden Memories; I Need This, Antiques!; The Kitchen Source; Lauren and Eddie Babbitt; Old America Stores; Pier 1 Imports; The Potting Shed; and Remember Then Antiques. Special thanks to Linda and Klaus Kranz for providing their kitchen for the photo shoot.

Page 135–137 constitutes an extension of this copyright page.

The text type was set in Adobe Garamond
The display type was set in Murray Hill
Composed in the United States of America
Designed by Nancy Rice Graphic Design
Edited by Tom Carpenter
Production supervised by Lisa Brownfield

Manufactured in Hong Kong by Global Interprint

FIRST IMPRESSION
ISBN 0-87358-614-x
Library of Congress Catalog Card Number Pending

Pictured on the cover: Griddled Elk Steak, page 21; Lynda's Baking Powder Biscuits, page 92.

0640/7.5M/6-97

This book is dedicated to the mountain men, soldiers, gunfighters, pioneers, dock hands, laborers, cattle barons, horsethieves, bank robbers, Yankees and Confederates, prostitutes and homemakers, all American Indian tribes, railroad builders, miners, the few honest frontier politicians, other legitimate liars, and all those who ever sighted down the barrel of a Hawken, Sharps, Remington, Winchester, Springfield, Spencer, Henry, Gatling, Hotchkiss, any matchlock or blunderbuss. Not forgetting those who supposedly fast-drew a Colt, Smith & Wesson, Derringer, or any other make of Old-West revolver, shotgun, or weapon of instant destruction. And, it's dedicated to the fiction writers (wonderful dreamers all), artists, photographers, and historians who have kept the genre(s) alive.

There are some types missing here and they deserve special attention, a chance to see the elephant you might say. Namely, I'd be remiss if I didn't mention the backbone to the real Old West. A tip of my John Batterson Stetson to all those souls who braved the forces of nature, the whine of an arrow, or the ricochet of a bullet to cook up a mess of vittles for the hands.

—B.W.

Contents

ABOUT WESTERN WRITERS OF AMERICA, BY R.C. HOUSE 1

SIERRA ADARE .... Jerky-Pingora Style 2
JUDY ALTER .... Mom McBain's Light Bread 4
SAM ARNOLD .... The Bowl of the Wife of Kit Carson 6
FRED BEAN .... Old-Fashioned Peach Cobbler 9
D. L. BIRCHFIELD .... Two-Skillet Campfire Cornbread 10
MIKE BLAKELY .... Chicken Pot Pie 12
CINDY BONNER .... Egg Gravy 14
MATT BRAUN .... Son-of-a-Bitch Stew 15
IRENE BENNETT BROWN .... Pioneer Corn Pudding 17
LARRY BROWN .... Griddled Elk Steaks 19
SINCLAIR BROWNING .... Snake Killer's Pozole 22
SUSAN BUTRUILLE .... Sunday Baked Beans 23
TONY CANO & ANN SOCHAT ...... Spicy Barbecue Drumsticks 24
LAURIE CARLSON .... Popcorn Balls 26
MURRAY CARROLL .... Hangtown Fry 27
PAUL CLAYTON .... Carne de Puerco (Shredded Pork) 30
RITA CLEARY .... Emma's Chokecherry Jelly 32
COLIN COBB .... Frybread 34
DON COLDSMITH .... Running Eagle's Beef Jerky 36
JAMES A. CRUTCHFIELD .... Peanut Soup 38
CHET CUNNINGHAM .... Deep-Fried Rattler 40
SHARON CUNNINGHAM .... Lou's Duck & Wild Rice 42
ANDREW DEQUASIE .... Faux Venison 44
JOHN DUNCKLEE .... Camarones Borrachos (Drunken Shrimp) 46
LOREN D. ESTLEMAN .... Tortilla Soup 48
JIM MARION ETTER .... Oklahoma-Style Fried Okra 50
ELIZABETH FACKLER .... Celsa's Chile Beans 52
PHYLLIS DE LA GARZA .... Stuffed Prickly Pear Leaves 54
KATHLEEN O'NEAL GEAR .... Wild Rice Pie 57
W. MICHAEL GEAR .... Roast Buffalo Hump 58
ROBIN GIBSON .... Cave Man Beans 61
CHARLES HACKENBERRY .... Milk Pie 62
STELLA HUGHES .... Vinegar Cobbler 64
SHARON IHLE .... Kate's Donegal Pie 66
JOHN JAKES .... Stuffed Roasted Cornish Game Hen 69
W. C. JAMESON .... Texas Brisket 72
FRED N. KIMMEL .... Venison Roast 74

ARTHUR WINFIELD KNIGHT ...... Homemade Butterscotch Ice Cream 76
RUTH WILLETT LANZA .... Shimázan's Lamb Stew 79
JOHN LEGG .... Apple Compote 81
ELMORE LEONARD .... Barbecued Guaymas Red Snapper 82
PRESTON LEWIS .... Gamma Lewis's Pecan Pie 84
ERNESTINE SEWELL LINCK .... Old-Fashioned Pound Cake 86
ELAINE LONG .... Green Beans with Pecan Sauce and Bacon 88
STAN LYNDE .... Lynda's Baking Powder Biscuits 91
KAT MARTIN .... Guisado Monterey (Monterey-Style Stew) 92
LARRY J. MARTIN .... Pozole and Pork Chops 94
JOE MEGEATH .... Savory Leg of Lamb 96
CANDY MOULTON .... Candy's Spudnuts 98
JOAN LOWERY NIXON .... Apple Butter 100
JIM PALMER .... Nine-Raisin Rice 102
CHORAL PEPPER .... Pepper's Dutch-Oven Cornbread Casserole 104
GWEN PETERSEN .... Sourdough Starter & Sourdough Pancakes 106
GEORGE POST .... One-Pot Chop Suey 108
ELLEN RECKNOR .... My Pecan Pie 110
JOYCE GIBSON ROACH .... Ranch-style Peach Cobbler 112
MARK ROBERTS .... Bocadillos Mejicanos (Mexican Appetizers) 114
JOANN ROE .... Prohibition Bean Dip 117
PATTI SHERLOCK .... Black Walnut and Ginger Shrimp Stir Fry 118
W. M. SHOCKLEY .... Pan-Fried Squirrel 120
RICHARD SLATTA .... Bunkhouse Beans 121
KATHRYN SWARTHOUT .... A Hill of Fried Potatoes 123
LON WALTERS .... Southwest Shoofly Pie 124
SANDY WHITING .... Fresh Strawberry Pie 125
JEANNE WILLIAMS .... Shaft's Burnt Sugar Cake 126
BOB WISEMAN .... Black Bean Frijoles 128
SALLY ZANJANI .... Goldfield Hotcakes for Two 129
NORM ZOLLINGER .... Sandwich from the Lake of the Little Shadows .. 131

ACKNOWLEDGMENTS 135
INDEX 138

About Western Writers of America

BY R.C. HOUSE

Western Writers of America, Inc., known to most of its nearly five hundred members simply as WWA, had its start in the early 1950s. Its development followed an exchange of letters between prolific Western novelist Nelson C. "Nels" Nye of Arizona, and the late Thomas "Tommy" Thompson of California, another versatile Western writer perhaps best known for his scripts for such TV series as *Rawhide, Gunsmoke, and Bonanza.*

1953 was a banner year for WWA as it adopted a constitution, elected officers, and began a treasury through dues assessment. Later, 1953 also saw establishment of the Spur awards program (sometimes erroneously referred to as the Golden Spur.)

Each year since, Spurs have been awarded for the publishing year's best Western books of fiction, nonfiction, juvenile fiction and nonfiction, and short fiction and nonfiction. Spurs for TV and film scripts were added in 1969 and 1971, and the Spur for cover art in 1981.

Another 1953 first was the introduction of the association's member publication, *Roundup.* Begun as a mimeographed newsletter edited by Nye, also WWA's first president, *Roundup* today is a professionally edited and designed magazine, drawing its content mainly from member contributions.

Administration of WWA's policies and programs is handled by volunteers; member officers and committee heads are elected or appointed.

Since 1954, WWA has held an annual convention—traditionally the last week in June—in a major city (selected by members) west of the Mississippi. Conventions offer opportunities for writer/editor/publisher interchanges, socializing and camaraderie, as well as workshops, panels, films and such, and visits to local historic sites. The crowning event of each convention is WWA's Spur Banquet, held on the convention's last evening. Spurs are awarded and so is the Owen Wister Award for lifelong contributions to the history and legends of the West and, since 1981, the Medicine Pipe Bearer's Award for the best first Western novel. Since 1984, the Stirrup Award has been given annually for the best contribution to *Roundup.*

Each year, as well, in a separate ceremony, two deceased Western writers are inducted into WWA's Hall of Fame, an honor based on outstanding contributions to the literature of the West.

WWA membership is divided into two categories, active and associate, under stipulations set forth in WWA's constitution. Generally, active members are working professionals with book and magazine credits. Associates may be newcomers to the Western writing field—editors, publishers, agents, artists, and writers still reaching for the goal of professional status.

Informally, WWA is characterized by its cherished traditions: *Roundup,* the Spurs, and the convention, which, for many hide-bound conventioneers, marks the end and the beginning of the year. WWA is also legendary for its intense yet often light-hearted convention hotel coffee shop, lounge, and hallway gabfests. It is these factors that keep WWA members bonded and bring conventioneers back year after year.

Sierra Adare, author of the award-winning book *What Editors Look For* (Cougar Imprints), *Backcountry Cooking* (Tamarack Books), and *Jackson Hole Uncovered* (Seaside Press), teaches and lectures on writing, marketing, cooking, and Native American topics, in addition to writing a syndicated book-review column. Her cooking, travel, and how-to articles have appeared in such national publications as *Persimmon Hill, Wild West, ByLine, Moccasin Telegraph, Mother Earth News,* and *Country Magazine*. She has contributed to five books, including *The Backcountry Handbook* (Simon and Schuster) and *NOLS Cookery* (National Outdoor Leadership School). Adare is active in Western Writers of America, Wordcraft Circle of Native Writers and Storytellers, Wyoming Writers, and Women Writing the West. Adare lives in Thermopolis, Wyoming.

EXCERPT FROM

Backcountry Cooking

Prior to 1900, people wandered through the wilderness for very different reasons. They searched for gold, fur, meat, or a better life, and they usually had a horse, mule, oxen, wagon, or handcart to carry their supplies.

Nowadays, backpacking trips range from an overnight experience to an excursion that lasts weeks.

We camp opposite of Pingora Peak, the most prominent formation in the Cirque of the Tower in Wyoming's Wind River Range. It ranks as a favorite for ambitious climbers, shooting up from Lonesome Lake like a gargantuan tree stump. Pingora derives its name from the Shoshone language and means "high, rocky, inaccessible peak."

We break camp and zigzag down Jackass Pass, stopping on the shore of North Lake to lunch among the boulders, sheltered from the ever-present wind—one of the elements the Cheyenne used in drying jerky. After cutting meat into thin strips, the women laid the pieces over bushes or on a hide, letting sun and air draw the moisture out of the meat. (The chore of keeping bugs and other things away from the meat fell on the children.) Once the meat dehydrated, the women packed it in parafleches—boxes made from heavy buffalo rawhide convenient for packing on a horse's back.

Published by Tamarack Books, Inc.

Jerky—Pingora Style

RECIPE COURTESY OF SIERRA ADARE

1 (16-ounce) beef roast	1 teaspoon onion powder
¼ cup soy sauce	1 teaspoon ginger, minced very fine
3 tablespoons Worcestershire sauce	(or ¼ tsp. powdered ginger)
3 tablespoons hickory-smoked salt	1 teaspoon Tabasco sauce
1 teaspoon garlic powder	1 teaspoon chili powder
1 teaspoon salt	

Partially freeze the roast and slice thin. (Freezing makes it easier to cut into thin strips, which allows for faster and more uniform drying.)

Mix together remaining ingredients to make the marinade.

Lay half the beef strips in a glass, 9 x 13-inch pan. (Avoid using a metal dish as it might give the meat a metallic taste; the larger surface area of this size pan allows you to distribute the marinade more evenly.)

Spoon the marinade over the meat. Repeat with another layer of beef strips and marinade. Cover with plastic wrap. Marinate 24 hours in the refrigerator.

Spread the slices on a foil-lined oven rack and dehydrate at 150°F for 8–12 hours or until dried, or use a home dehydrator, using the machine's instructions. Store in airtight containers in the refrigerator or freezer.

Judy Alter writes primarily historical fiction about women in the American West, writing both for the adult market and young adults. Her works include *Cherokee Rose* (Bantam); *Mattie* (Doubleday 1987 Spur Award winner for Best Western Novel of the Year), *"Fool Girl,"* a short story that won a Western Heritage Wrangler Award from the National Cowboy Hall of Fame; and *Luke and the Van Sandt County War,* named the Best Young Adult Novel of 1984 by the Texas Institute of Letters. Other recent novels are *Libbie,* about Elizabeth Bacon Custer (Mrs. George Armstrong Custer), and *Jessie,* about Jessie Benton Fremont (Mrs. John Charles Fremont). Alter lives in Fort Worth, Texas.

⇒•◇•⇐

EXCERPT FROM

CHEROKEE ROSE

"Sandy!" she exclaimed in surprise, using the name that everyone but Mama called him. Then her eyes rested on me, and she stood speechless, looking at him.

"This is Tommy Jo, my daughter. She's goin' to stay with you a week," he said. There was no asking in his statement; it was foregone that she would do as he wished.

"Of course, Tommy Jo. I'm glad to know you. I'm Louise Turner." She never lost her composure, after that first minute of surprise. . . .

"Do you cook?" she asked.

"Yes. Mama taught me. I can make bread and pies and pretty good mayonnaise."

This time her laughter burbled gently. "Good. When we need mayonnaise in the middle of winter, I'll let you know. Meantime, you can stir the stew, and I'll see about the bread. It's already rising, or I'd let you show me what you can do."

Dinner was delicious—hearty stew filled with chunks of beef, potatoes, carrots and onions, bread fresh from the oven and as light as any I'd ever tasted, and an apple cobbler for dessert. Even the coffee smelled so good that I was tempted to taste it—Mama never allowed me to at home, saying it would stunt my growth. One bitter sip convinced me that Mama was right.

Published by Bantam Books

⇒•◇•⇐

Mom McBain's Light Bread

RECIPE COURTESY OF JUDY ALTER

2 cups milk
2 cups warm water
2 packages dry yeast
4 tablespoons plus ½ teaspoon sugar

2 teaspoons salt
5 tablespoons vegetable oil
12 cups flour

Scald the milk. Add to milk all but ½ cup of the water. Sprinkle yeast into remaining ½ cup water and add the ½ teaspoon sugar to hasten yeast process. Let yeast mix rise for 10 minutes.

In a large mixing bowl, combine milk mixture, remaining sugar, salt, vegetable oil, and 2 cups of the flour. Add softened yeast mixture and blend in. Add enough of the remaining flour to make a moderately stiff dough. (Don't worry if you don't use all of the flour. If there's not *enough* flour, add more in ½-cup increments.)

Turn out dough on a lightly floured surface (countertop, large cutting board, or dough board); knead until smooth and satiny (about 8–10 minutes). Shape dough into a ball; place in a lightly greased bowl, turning once to grease surface. Cover and let rise in a warm place until double (about 1½ hours).

Punch dough down. Let rise again until double (45 minutes).

Cut dough in two portions. Shape each into a smooth ball. Cover and let rest 10 minutes. Shape dough in loaves and place in two greased loaf pans. Cover each pan with a dry towel and let bread rise until double (about 1 hour).

Preheat oven to 400°F.

Bake for 10 minutes. Without opening the oven, lower temperature to 350°F and bake for 35–40 minutes.

Sam Arnold, in addition to having a busy writing career, is owner of the prestigious Fort Restaurant—a replica of the 1834 Bent's Fort, confirmed as one of the Old West's first fur-trading posts—near Morrison, Colorado.

Arnold has authored several culinary/historical books including *Eating Up the Santa Fe Trail* (University Press of Colorado) and *Fryingpans West,* and was author/spokesman for *Coors Taste of the West Cookbook* for eight years. He also hosted and produced regional and national television shows such as *Food For Thought, Fryingpans West TV,* and *Feast of Life.*

Arnold studied with James Beard, entertained Julia Child, and has been featured in national publications and television programs, including *The New York Times, Modern Maturity, People Magazine, Bon Appetit, Gourmet, Americana, Newsday, Today,* ABC and NBC news, CNN, TNN, *Discovery,* and *Live with Regis and Kathy Lee.*

His latest book is *The Fort Restaurant: New Foods of the Old West* (HarperCollins). Arnold lives in Morrison, Colorado.

⇒•◇•⇐

EXCERPT FROM

THE FORT RESTAURANT: NEW FOODS OF THE OLD WEST

In the spring of 1961, two years before opening The Fort, my family and I found ourselves stopped, during a trip to Mexico, in Durango, some 600 miles south of the border in Mexico, driving a tiny English Morris Mini-minor. Today a city of several hundred thousand, it was then less than half that size. We were told the best place to eat was the drugstore. Following that lead the next morning, we watched a stream of young children coming in from the fields to fill family lunch buckets with a special soup. It smelled so good that we tried it.

The bowls we were served held a heady, spicy broth of chicken, with nice bites of white cheese. The secret of its great taste, though, was the chipotle chiles, smoked jalapeños, that gave the soup a distinctive bite and delicious smoky flavor.

Caldo Tlapeno was its proper name, we learned, and when The Fort opened, it went on the menu. Nobody could pronounce it (nor knew what it meant), so it didn't sell until one day, Leona Wood, the septuagenarian who ran our gift shop trade room on weekends, exclaimed, "I remember my grandmother serving us this dish!" Miss Wood happened to be the last granddaughter of Kit Carson and so, "The Bowl of the Wife of Kit Carson" was christened. For 35 years it has been a signature dish of The Fort.

Published by HarperCollins

⇒•◇•⇐

The Bowl of the Wife of Kit Carson,
page 8

The Bowl of the Wife of Kit Carson

RECIPE COURTESY OF SAM ARNOLD

2 whole chicken breasts, boned and skinned
1 quart chicken broth
pinch of dried Mexican-leaf oregano
1 cup rice, cooked
1 cup garbanzo beans, cooked (preferably from dried)
1 ripe avocado, peeled, pitted, and chopped
1 chipotle chile, in adobo sauce, minced
1 cup Monterey Jack or Havarti cheese, cubed
4 sprigs cilantro

Place the chicken breasts in a pot with the broth. Bring to a boil, then turn off the heat and cover for 12 minutes to poach the chicken gently.

Remove the chicken and cut into strips 1½ inches wide. Add to the broth the oregano and the chicken strips along with the rice, garbanzos, avocado, and chipotle chile.

Divide the cheese among 4 deep soup bowls.

Quickly heat the soup again to a rapid boil, then ladle into the bowls. Garnish each with a cilantro sprig.

Fred Bean's first novel, *Tom Spoon*, was published by Walker and Company. Since then Bean has been writing at a whirlwind pace and has produced *Hard Luck* and *Gunfight at Eagle Springs*, also for Walker; *Bloody Sunday, Killing Season, Renegade,* and *Range War* for Fawcett Gold Medal; *Cry of the Wolf, The Last Warrior, The Outlaw, Law of the Gun, Trails End,* and several more for Zebra Books; *Pancho and Black Jack* for Simon & Schuster; and *Rivers West: Pecos River* for Bantam Books. Bean lives in Austin, Texas.

EXCERPT FROM

TRAILS END

The fire provided warmth from an October night chill in the Nations. Men were seated around the flames, palming cups of coffee as the hour grew late. Cookie had prepared a feast of fried potatoes and cornbread, topped off by a peach cobbler made from tins of sweet peaches he bought in Fort Worth, flavored with cinnamon.

Published by Zebra Books

Old-Fashioned Peach Cobbler

RECIPE COURTESY OF FRED BEAN

½ cup butter
1 cup self-rising flour
1 cup milk
¾ cup sugar

1 (16-ounce) can sliced peaches
 in heavy syrup
1 teaspoon ground cinnamon

Preheat oven to 350°F.

In a glass or ceramic bowl mix together flour, milk, and sugar and pour into Dutch oven or large skillet.

Combine peaches and syrup with cinnamon and add to flour mixture. Dot with pats of remaining butter.

Heat the Dutch oven on top of the stove until a drop of water quickly sizzles away, then add half of the butter and swirl to coat.

Remove from stove and bake in the oven for 30–35 minutes or until crust rises and turns golden brown.

Author D. L. Birchfield is a member of the Choctaw Nation of Oklahoma and a graduate of the University of Oklahoma College of Law. He has written five children's books, co-edited an anthology of Native American poetry, served on the editorial staffs of a number of publications, and was general editor of a ten-volume encyclopedia of North American Indians. His short story "Never Again" was among those selected to appear in the anthology *Blue Dawn, Red Earth: New Native American Storytellers* (Doubleday Anchor Books). He is copy editor for *Roundup Magazine* (WWA). In 1996–97 he was a visiting faculty member at Cornell University, teaching American Indian literature. Birchfield lives in Oklahoma City, Oklahoma.

EXCERPT FROM

NEVER AGAIN

"This is as far as I'm going," said Delbert. "If we camp here at least maybe we'll be able to find our way back. Dad never will stop laughing if he finds out we got off up here and got lost."

The little creek had just enough water flowing in it to use it for camp water, so we followed it downstream until we found a good place to camp. We pitched camp and then went out hunting until it got dark.

We hadn't seen a deer all day, and we weren't real sure where we were, but that didn't dampen our spirits. It was a beautiful evening, and a big supper cooked over a campfire tasted pretty good.

We sat around drinking coffee, just enjoying the evening and the campfire, until finally we spread out that old tarp, rolled out our sleeping bags on top of it, and bedded down.

Published by Anchor Books

◆ 10 ◆   D.L. BIRCHFIELD

Two-Skillet Campfire Cornbread

RECIPE COURTESY OF D. L. BIRCHFIELD

This is an outdoor recipe you can use when camping. To make this cornbread at home, use the same procedures and keep the heat at medium (not too high). You will need two cast-iron skillets for this recipe.

1 tablespoon lard or shortening	*1 egg*
1 cup cornmeal, self-rising	*¾ cup water*

In one cast-iron skillet melt the lard. Pour the melted lard into the other iron skillet. Use the lard to grease the insides of both skillets. Pour the remaining lard off in a deep mixing bowl; set the skillets aside.

In the mixing bowl combine the lard, cornmeal, egg, and water to form a batter. Pour the batter into one of the skillets, then place the other skillet, upside down, over the top to form a high lid.

The cornbread requires a lower cooking temperature than the campfire provides. Place the skillet on a bed of coals a few feet from the fire.

Cook for 10–15 minutes or until batter has become firm and is beginning to brown along the edges of the skillet. Carefully turn the skillets upside down and continue cooking until the cornbread is cooked to your taste.

Set the cornbread aside, wrapped in a towel to keep it warm, rinse out the skillets, and use them to cook the rest of the meal.

Mike Blakely's *Shortgrass Song* was a WWA Spur Finalist for the Best Novel of the Year in 1994. He currently has a multiple-book contract with Forge. His latest books are *Snowy Range Gang* and *Too Long at the Dance*. Blakely lives in Marble Falls, Texas.

EXCERPT FROM

SHORTGRASS SONG

"Ladies and gentlemen," the captain said, "General William Jackson Palmer sends his regards to this gathering of loyal Union fighting men. The general regrets he could not attend himself. However, on behalf of the Denver and Rio Grande Railroad, the Fountain Colony, the city of Colorado Springs, and General Palmer himself, my daughter, Amelia, and I are pleased to present to this reunion of patriotic souls a grand and lavish feast! Behold!" and the captain swept his hand toward the plains.

Down the road from Colorado Springs came a regular processional of supply wagons, prompting a gasp and a cheer to issue from the crowd. The wagons were met by former troopers who galloped out to escort them to the reunion grounds. They carried chefs who would serve raw oysters, mock turtle soup, Mackinaw trout in egg sauce, boiled leg of mutton in caper sauce, roast loin of beef with oyster dressing, glazed sweetbreads, baked chicken pie, boiled potatoes, mashed potatoes, sweet potatoes, peas, tomatoes, spinach, celery, and olives. One wagon hauled nothing but watermelons. Another, the box of which was lined with ice, carried pies, cakes, puddings, and custards of every description.

The rest of the day favored the speechmakers, as the gluttons rendered indolent by the feast fell to lounging about the arbors. And every orator who stood before his old comrades sang the praises of Ab Holcomb, generous reunion host and hero of Apache Canyon.

Published by Forge

Chicken Pot Pie

RECIPE COURTESY OF MIKE BLAKELY

1 large roasting chicken
2 cups carrots (4–5 medium-sized), sliced
1 cup chopped onion
2 stalks celery, chopped, with leaves
bouquet garni (6 parsley sprigs, 1 bay leaf, tied together)
¼ teaspoon thyme
1 cup mushroom caps, quartered
salt and white pepper to taste
½ cup beer, at room temperature
2 tablespoons butter
½ cup heavy cream, whipped
2 tablespoons flour
12 ounces puff pastry (fresh or frozen)
1 egg yolk, beaten

Put chicken and enough hot water to cover it in a large, deep kettle or Dutch oven. Add carrots, onion, celery, and bouquet garni. Bring to a boil. Skim residue from kettle. Reduce to a simmer, cover, and let cook for 15–20 minutes. Remove from heat and let cool for 1 hour, then pour into a large mixing bowl. Reserve broth in a bowl after removing carrots, onion, and celery; leave the bouquet garni in the broth.

Joint chicken and remove meat from bones; discard bones and skin (or add back to broth and let simmer for a few hours until you have a nice, rich broth for other uses). Cut meat into large serving pieces.

Preheat oven to 400°F.

To a deep pie or casserole dish add chicken, carrots, onion, celery, thyme, mushrooms, salt and pepper, and beer. Cut butter into small pieces and dabble over chicken mix. Mix flour into whipped cream, making sure there are no lumps, then pour evenly over chicken.

Roll out puff pastry and place in pie dish or casserole dish. Brush top with beaten egg yolk.

Bake in oven for 10 minutes, then reduce heat to 350°F and bake for 20 more minutes.

Cindy Bonner's first novel, *Lily,* was a finalist for the WWA Medicine Pipe Bearer's Award for Best First Novel of the West. Both *Lily* and *Looking After Lily* were named Best Adult Books for Young Adults by the American Library Association. *The Passion of Dellie O'Barr,* the third book in her McDade Cycle, is now available from Algonquin Books of Chapel Hill, North Carolina. Bonner is currently working on a fourth novel, set during World War I and the 1920s. Bonner lives in Yorktown, Texas.

EXCERPT FROM

LOOKING AFTER LILY

Lily had a fire glowing, and coffee brewing. Em laid on a quilt spread down on the ground to make a pallet, and she rested content, watching her ma make gravy out of nothing, a little lard, flour, and chopped-up boiled eggs.

"You ain't well yet," Lily said, glancing at me as I sat up. She poured me a cup of coffee, spooned in some goat's milk. "I heard you shivering all night."

I took the cup and wrapped my hands around it. The morning damp was on the air. She sliced a cold biscuit in half, laid it on the tin plate, and ladled the egg gravy over the top. She handed me that too, and a fork.

"You can rest in the wagon," she said. "We've got level road through here. I'll drive the mule."

I forked in a bite and shook my head, but not because I didn't like her suggestion. What I was thinking of was how good the food tasted, and how I couldn't seem to fill up. Like I had a yawning pit open in my belly.

She frowned at me. "I can drive a mule, she said. "I've done it plenty. . . . "

Published by Algonquin Books of Chapel Hill

Egg Gravy

RECIPE COURTESY OF CINDY BONNER

Serve over biscuits or toast.

2 tablespoons lard
2 tablespoons flour
2 cups milk

salt and pepper to taste
4–6 eggs, hard-boiled and coarsely
  chopped

Melt lard in a skillet over medium heat. Stir in flour until smooth and bubbling. Slowly add milk, stirring constantly. Bring to a boil to thicken. Season with salt and pepper. Add chopped eggs and heat through.

Matt Braun won the WWA Spur Award for his historical novel *The Kincaids*. He has over forty published books, with over thirty-six million copies in print. His novels have been published in eleven foreign languages. Braun lives in Winstead, Connecticut.

EXCERPT FROM

THE SAVAGE LAND

Doughbelly Ketchum was king around the chuck wagon, and according to some, a tyrant. Like most cow outfit cooks, the head pot-walloper of Sunburst considered himself one of the anointed few, answerable only to God. He had certain rules for those who frequented his picnic grounds, and woe be unto the hands' stomachs if anybody stepped out of line. His dictates were followed to the letter.

There were certain advantages to the arrangement. Namely, the scrumptious meals Doughbelly could whip up if the mood struck him. Perhaps because his beloved chuck wagon had made it safely across the Red, he was in fine fettle this particular night. When the hands lined up with their tin plates they found themselves presented with a princely feast. Son-of-a-bitch stew, which consisted of loins, sweetbreads, liver and heart simmered in a spicy gravy. Spotted Pup, a racy combination of rice, raisins and brown sugar. Sourdough biscuits and molasses. Dried apple pie sprinkled with cinnamon. And that old standby, without which no feast was ever complete, six-shooter coffee.

Doughbelly had outdone himself. The hands dug in with an assortment of grunts, slurps and appreciative belches.

Published by Popular Library

Son-of-a-Bitch Stew

RECIPE COURTESY OF MATT BRAUN

This is a favorite with old-time cowboys across the West. Be aware that without marrow gut it is not a true Son-of-a-Bitch. Your friendly butcher can supply all of the parts originally collected by a bunkhouse cook. Once you try this stew with marrow gut, you'll never again question the culinary skills of those Old West chuck-wagon cooks.

1 pound beef steak
¼ pound beef fat
¾ pound beef heart
½ pound beef liver
1 marrow gut
½ pound sweetbreads

1 pound beef brains
salt and black pepper to taste
generous dash of cayenne
2 tablespoons flour
water as needed

Cut all beef parts into 1-inch cubes. Place everything except brains and seasoning into large stew pot and add water to cover twice over. Cook on low heat for four hours; add water if necessary to keep slightly covered.

Add brains, salt, black pepper, and cayenne. Simmer for 30 minutes and then thicken broth with flour and ½ cup water. If not spicy hot, add more cayenne.

Irene Bennett Brown's novel *The Plainswoman* was a 1994 WWA Spur Award Finalist for Best Original Western Paperback. Her *Before the Lark* won a WWA Spur Award for Best Western Juvenile Book in 1984. Brown lives in Jefferson, Oregon.

THE PLAINSWOMAN

"The sun was noon-high when the doors of her house and barn were removed temporarily from their hinges and placed across barrels to form tables in the yard. Huge pots of beans, kettles of boiled beef and noodles, sauerkraut with pork, corn pudding, corn dodgers, corn on the cob, corn cake, and hominy, were brought out. Joe Samuel laughingly praised God for corn, then asked His help with this year's doubtful crop. Which prompted one ranch wife to report with a touch of rancor that her collection of recipes using corn numbered thirty-three and her husband to add that he once went a three-year stretch with no other bread except cornbread to eat. Many eyes turned to the sky, then, with Mr. Bergen wondering aloud for all of them. 'We get all the rain we going to get this summer, I wonder?'"

Published by Ballantine Books

Pioneer Corn Pudding
RECIPE COURTESY OF IRENE BENNETT BROWN

1½ cups corn, fresh kernels or plain canned	½ teaspoon nutmeg
4 eggs, separated	1 teaspoon vanilla
½ cup sugar	¼ teaspoon salt
1 teaspoon cinnamon	butter for baking dish
	whipped cream

Preheat oven to 375°F.

In a blender combine corn and egg yolks. Add sugar, cinnamon, nutmeg, vanilla, and salt.

Beat egg whites until they peak. Fold egg whites thoroughly into the corn mixture. Pour into a buttered, 1-quart baking or soufflé dish.

Bake for 25–30 minutes or until top is firm when touched.

Serve immediately with whipping cream.

Pioneer Corn Pudding,
page 17

Larry Brown has written over eight hundred articles in publications such as *Wild West, True West, Old West, Wyoming Annals, Wyoming History Journal,* and many other publications. He researched and scripted a two-hour *Today* show as well as a one-hour *Prime Time Sunday* program broadcast. His *Hog Ranches of Wyoming: Liquor, Lust & Lies Under Sagebrush Skies* received the Western Horizon Award from Wyoming Writers. His latest book, *You are Respectfully Invited to Attend My Execution* (High Plains Press), contains little-known stories of the seven men who were legally executed in Wyoming Territory. Brown lives in Cheyenne, Wyoming.

EXCERPT FROM

HOG RANCHES OF WYOMING: LIQUOR, LUST & LIES UNDER SAGEBRUSH SKIES

It seems I was just in time for breakfast, for . . . the girls did not get up early, and I of course, joined them being and always hungry. Jack Sanders was sitting at the head of the table with Vi alongside. There were two other men besides myself, and as I remember six girls?

It was a nice meal, baking powder biscuits, fired meat, Arbuckles coffee, etc. . . . The meat was on one large platter and was passed around. After eating awhile, someone said, "Please pass the beef."

When Jack Sanders heard this he said, "This is elk." . . . Pretty soon someone at the other end of the table said, "Please pass the beef." Pulling out his six gun and shooting into the ceiling he [Sanders] said, "I said this is elk" and from the end of the table came a calm voice saying, "Would you please pass the elk?"

Published by High Plains Press

Griddled Elk Steaks

RECIPE COURTESY OF LARRY BROWN

4 elk sirloin steaks, 1 inch thick	¼ cup olive oil
¼ cup soy sauce	½ teaspoon white pepper
2 cloves garlic, minced	¼ cup balsamic vinegar
1 teaspoon minced fresh ginger	4 tablespoons Cajun-style seasoning
¼ cup Bordeaux wine, or burgundy	4 tablespoons butter

Remove all fat from elk steaks.

To make marinade, in a blender mix thoroughly the soy sauce, garlic, ginger, wine, olive oil, white pepper, and balsamic vinegar.

In a deep, glass or ceramic bowl, pour ¼ of the marinade, then add the steaks and remaining marinade; thoroughly coat the steaks. Cover and marinate at room temperature for two hours.

Remove the steaks from marinade. Drain, reserving garlic and ginger. Pat the steaks dry, then rub both sides with Cajun seasoning.

Bring a large, deep skillet to moderate heat. Melt 2 tablespoons butter until lightly frothy, then add the reserved garlic and ginger.

Fry two steaks at a time for about 3 minutes per side before turning (use tongs, not a fork). Fry other side for 3 minutes for rare, or 4 minutes for medium (never serve venison-style meats well done). Repeat process for two remaining steaks.

Griddled Elk Steak

Sinclair Browning is the author of *Lyons on Horses* (Doubleday), *America's Best* (AMC), and *Enju: The Life and Struggle of an Apache Chief from the Little Running Water* (Northland Press). Her *Ounce of Prevention* column frequently appears in *Performance Horse* magazine. Browning lives in Tucson, Arizona.

EXCERPT FROM

ENJU: THE LIFE AND STRUGGLE OF AN APACHE CHIEF FROM THE LITTLE RUNNING WATER

Rations were issued every Saturday morning. They consisted of three hundred pounds of beef, fifty pounds of flour, eight pounds of sugar, four pounds of coffee, and one pound of salt for every one hundred Indians. The beef was issued "on the hoof," for in this way the Apaches could utilize every bit of the animal, including the hide and the marrow in the tiniest bones.

Published by Northland Press

Snake Killer's Pozole

RECIPE COURTESY OF SINCLAIR BROWNING

This recipe always tastes better the next day.

2 tablespoons olive oil
1 onion, chopped
2 cloves garlic, chopped
3–5 cups beef or chicken broth
   (depending on which meat
   is used)
½ teaspoon pepper
½ teaspoon cumin
½ teaspoon cloves
½ teaspoon cayenne
1 (29-ounce) can hominy
1 (29-ounce) can tomatoes,
   chopped
1 (4-ounce) can chiles, diced
1½ pounds cooked meat
   (pork, beef, turkey, chicken)

Heat a Dutch oven or large, deep pot until a drop of water quickly sizzles away. Add the olive oil and saute the onion and garlic. Add the broth, pepper, cumin, cloves, cayenne, hominy, tomatoes, chiles, and meat. Cook, covered, at a low simmer for 45–60 minutes.

Susan Butruille is the author of *Women's Voices from the Oregon Trail* and *Women's Voices from the Western Frontier,* both published by Tamarack Books, Inc. Butruille, a public speaker as well as an editor and writer, lives in Portland, Oregon.

WOMEN'S VOICES FROM THE OREGON TRAIL

Women learned to settle in as fast as they could because they didn't know how long they'd be there.

That first winter, the families survived on whatever food they could get: salmon and potatoes, boiled wheat and peas, milk, butter, deer meat, and coffee from dried wheat, barley, or peas, ground in coffee mills.

Sunday became a traditional visiting day, and a woman would have to guess how many places to set for the Sunday meal, not knowing who might come visiting. . . .

Some pioneer women were not thrilled about having company to cook for. "Mr. B is agoing to have his house raised and I have got to get dinner for about twenty persons besides being bothered with two lady visitors," wrote America Rollins Butler in the Rogue River Valley in 1853. Later, she wrote that "dinner is over and I am hartly glad of it for I never did like to cook."

Published by Tamarack Books, Inc.

Sunday Baked Beans

RECIPE COURTESY OF SUSAN BUTRUILLE, ADAPTED FROM
"CROSS SECTION OF PIONEER LIFE AT FOURTH PLAIN,"
BY ELIZABETH GEDNEY, *OREGON HISTORICAL QUARTERLY,* XLIII
(MARCH/DECEMBER 1942).

This recipe is as it was described in the 1942 article. Make your own guess at how many pounds and what type(s) of beans to use, as well as the quantities of salt pork and molasses.

Soak beans over Friday night and boil them on Saturday morning until, when you take some in a spoon and blow on them, the shells split. Put the soaked beans into a big pot between layers of salt pork. Pour molasses over all and bake until noon Sunday.

El Paso writers Tony Cano and Ann Sochat have co-authored two books: *Dutch Oven Cooking with Tony Cano* and *Echoes in the Wind: Ranch Recollections and Poetry.*

Cano is a former designer and manufacturer of jackets for many famous personalities in the entertainment industry, professional and amateur rodeo circuits, Formula One and NASCAR racing teams, universities and corporate America.

Sochat, a teacher in the El Paso School District and at the El Paso County Community College, performs at cowboy and Western heritage symposiums. Her poems have been published in *Western Horseman Magazine* and the *Western Horseman Buying Guide.* Sochat is a member of the Texas Cowboy Poets Society.

EXCERPT FROM

DUTCH OVEN COOKING WITH TONY CANO

CHUCKWAGON CHARLEY

You will read about the heroes of those famous cattle trails,
Of the wranglers in the spaces wide and free,
And you'll read about the cowboys and their days upon the range,
But you'll never read a word of praise 'bout me.
Fer I never rode no bronc ner dressed in spurs and Stetson hat,
And that is why I always get the snub,
But I was most important to those long, hard cattle drives
Cause I'm Charley, the man who cooks the grub.

I was the first man to be awake, to get the fire going,
And the last man to finish work at night.
When it comes to feedin' hungry men, the cookin's never done.
You need lots of food and you better fix it right!
Cookin', bakin', fryin', boilin', mixin', gratin', stirrin', mashin',
Choppin', peelin' wore my fingers to the nub,
But their clean plates said they liked it, and every now and then,
One of them would say, "Thanks, Charley, fer the grub!"

So I never will be famous in the annals of the West
Ner a member of the cowboy heroes' club,
But no cavalry or roundup could have traveled very far
Without Charley, the man who cooks the grub!

—Ann Sochat

Published by Reata Publishing Company

Spicy Barbecue Drumsticks

RECIPE COURTESY OF TONY CANO

This recipe can be cooked outdoors over coals or at home in the oven.

2 tablespoons vegetable oil, plus enough to coat cooking pot
1 (12-inch) Dutch oven (or large Pyrex dish, if cooked indoors)
40 charcoal briquets—27 to start, 13 to replenish
3 pounds chicken drumsticks or wing pieces
salt and pepper
1 cup honey
½ cup soy sauce
½ clove garlic, chopped
2 tablespoons catsup

Outdoor method:

Lightly oil Dutch oven and set up to cook with 9 hot briquets underneath.

Arrange chicken drumsticks in Dutch oven. Sprinkle with oil, salt, and pepper.

In a small bowl, combine honey, soy sauce, garlic, and catsup. Pour over the drumsticks, coating all sides evenly.

Cover and bake for 1 hour with 18 briquets on the lid. You will need to replenish the coals at the end of the first hour by placing four fresh briquets on the bottom and nine fresh briquets on the lid. Bake for another 30–45 minutes or until chicken is thoroughly cooked and the sauce has caramelized (when the sauce has thickened and turned the chicken pieces a dark brown).

Oven method:

Preheat oven to 375°F.

In a Pyrex dish, prepare the the chicken as described above.

Bake, uncovered, for 1½ hours or until chicken is thoroughly cooked and sauce has caramelized.

L aurie Carlson, an award-winning writer of children's books, writes what she terms kids activity books. Her titles include *Kid's Camp!*, *Westward Ho!*, *More Than Moccasins*, *EcoArt!*, and *Kids Create!*, all published by Chicago Review Press. Carlson lives in Cheney, Washington.

WESTWARD HO!

Corn was one of the most easily grown crops in homesteaders' fields and gardens. American Indians had been growing it for a long time in their gardens when they introduced it to the European explorers. Within a short time, everyone in North America was eating something made from corn. Here's a tasty treat to make from popcorn, that would have been very popular at frontier parties. In those days it would have been made with molasses; here's an easy way to do it.

Published by Chicago Review Press

Popcorn Balls

RECIPE COURTESY OF LAURIE CARLSON

1 gallon popped corn (about ½ cup before popping)
60 caramels, unwrapped
¼ cup water

Put popcorn in a large bowl.

Heat the caramels and water in a saucepan over medium-low heat, stirring continually. When the caramels are melted and the mixture is smooth, pour it over the popcorn. Mix to coat.

Using your hands, shape the popcorn mixture into balls the size of baseballs. The caramel won't stick to your hands if you keep them wet. Place the popcorn balls on waxed paper. They will be firm in about an hour; sooner if you put them in the refrigerator to chill.

This recipe makes about 16 popcorn balls. To store them, put each popcorn ball in a separate plastic sandwich bag.

Murray Carroll has written for *True West Magazine, Old West Magazine, The Annals of Wyoming, Journal of the National Association for Outlaws and Lawmen Historical Society,* and *Journal of the Western Association for Outlaws and Lawmen Historical Society.* In addition, he has many pieces in news media around the west. Carroll lives in Anacortes, Washington.

EXCERPT FROM

THE PERIPATETIC OYSTER

Down in Hangtown, the chef at the Cary House made a permanent addition to American cuisine. A recently successful miner came into the hotel dining room and demanded the most expensive dish in the house. The most costly ingredients available were eggs and oysters, so the cook prepared a mixture of eggs, oysters, and bacon. It is not improbable that the cook was Chinese and simply prepared an oyster foo yung. No matter, even after Hangtown became more genteel Placerville, Hangtown Fry remained a favorite dish there, as well as throughout the western mining world.

Published by True West Magazine

Hangtown Fry

Hangtown Fry

RECIPE COURTESY OF MURRAY CARROLL

½ pint oysters, extra small
½ cup flour
1 tablespoon water
3 large eggs, beaten
½ cup cornmeal, preferably
   stone-ground

4 strips bacon, thick
½ teaspoon finely grated onion
¼ teaspoon salt
course-ground black pepper,
   to taste

Drain oysters, pat dry, and roll in flour. Mix the water with the beaten eggs. Roll oysters in the egg mixture, then in the cornmeal. Set the oysters aside to "rest" for about a half hour.

In a cast-iron skillet, fry the bacon until it's crisp. Place bacon strips on paper towels. Drain most of the bacon grease from the skillet. Brown the oysters and onion in the remaining grease.

Crumble the bacon and add to skillet. Pour remaining egg mixture into skillet and stir to mix evenly. Add salt and pepper.

Cook until mixture is firm and bottom is lightly browned.

Serve with cornbread or biscuits.

Paul Clayton is currently working on a series on the early contacts between the Muskogee people of the Southeast and the Spanish, French, and English colonials. His titles include *Calling Crow, Calling Crow Nation,* and *Flight of the Crow.* Clayton lives in south San Francisco, California.

CALLING CROW

Calling Crow shoveled dirt into the woman's basket. "Are you of the Guale People?" she asked; he didn't hear her. He, like the others in the pit, was entranced by the smell wafting over them, and could think of nothing else. The smell came from the bank where Spanish guards roasted an animal over a fire. Everyone knew it was for the Spanish only; never had they given the People meat, except once when some rotten scraps were mixed in with their cassava bread. People told Calling Crow this animal was a pig. All morning the sweet scent of the pig meat and the crisp smell of its fat dripping onto the fire tickled and teased everyone's nostrils cruelly until meat was all anyone could think about. They talked of it in angry, muffled tones; older, weaker ones even wept as they worked. Calling Crow thought that No-Neck, who worked close by, would go mad. He had not taken his eyes off of it and had fallen down several times because he had been walking backwards to keep the pig in sight. Two Spanish pointed at Calling Crow, No-Neck and an old man called Big Heart. "You three! Come with me."

Published by Berkley Publishing Group

Carne de Puerco (Shredded Pork)

RECIPE COURTESY OF PAUL CLAYTON

Carne de puerco is shredded pork (machaca) that may be used as a filling for tacos, enchiladas, tamales, or any recipe that calls for shredded meat.

⅓ pound pork tenderloin	1 cup malt vinegar
¼ teaspoon cumin	½ cup olive oil
¼ teaspoon nutmeg	1 cup guava nectar
¼ teaspoon oregano	1 cup pineapple juice
¼ teaspoon chili powder	4 cloves garlic, minced
¼ teaspoon white pepper	¼ teaspoon salt
6 whole mild green chiles, canned	

Rinse the pork tenderloin and pat dry with a paper towel. Remove fat. Make several shallow crosswise cuts in the meat.

In a mortar, combine cumin, nutmeg, oregano, chili powder, and white pepper. Grind to release flavors and mix spices. Rub the meat with the spice mixture, place it in a deep glass or ceramic casserole dish, and set aside.

To make marinade, in a blender combine green chiles, malt vinegar, olive oil, guava nectar, pineapple juice, garlic, and salt. Pour mix over pork and marinate at room temperature for 1 hour.

Preheat oven to 350°F.

Coat pork with marinade and bake for 2 hours. Remove and let cool in juices. Remove pork to a large cutting board and pat dry. Pour off juices (or reserve for other uses such as gravy). With a fork, shred meat finely. Place shredded pork in a casserole dish and return to oven; bake at 350°F for 20–30 minutes or until crisp on top.

Rita Cleary, the daughter of a Metropolitan Opera ballerina, was born in New York City. She is the author of many magazine articles and has authored several books, among them *Sorrel* and *Goldtown*, published by Sunstone Press (Santa Fe, New Mexico). "Sidesaddle," a short story, was published by *Steamboat Magazine*. Cleary is presently working on a Revolutionary War story during which Long Island was occupied by the British. Rita Cleary lives near the ocean at Oyster Bay, New York.

⟫─◆─⟪

EXCERPT FROM

GOLDTOWN

Emma arrived with lunch and Lysaght stopped abruptly. She placed a tray of bread, cheese, chokecherry jam and coffee on the table when they heard a wagon pull up. There was a knock at the door and the sound of boots and the pungent smell of a cigar. It was McGillicuddy.

"Race day, Emma. You coming?"

Emma Dubois had never missed Sunday afternoon at the races but today she had completely forgotten. She hurried to get ready.

McGillicuddy nodded to Lysaght but addressed Cameron, "You're welcome to come too."

"Thanks, but I'm hungry." The food looked too good to pass up. "I wouldn't want to sully the lady's reputation further." He smothered a slice of bread with chokecherry jam, sliced a wedge of cheese on top and poured himself a cup of coffee. "If you'll excuse me, I'm going to have a good meal and a good look at a good horse." He sat down and offered a plate to Lysaght. He hoped he hadn't offended McGillicuddy, but Emma would understand.

Published by Sunstone Press

⟫─◆─⟪

Emma's Chokecherry Jelly

RECIPE COURTESY OF RITA CLEARY

3½ lbs. chokecherries
3 cups water

6½ cups sugar
1 (6-ounce) bottle of liquid pectin

Wash chokecherries.

Place in a deep mixing bowl and crush to release juice. In a large pot combine chokecherries and water. Bring to a boil, then reduce heat and simmer for 15 minutes.

Drain the juice into a large glass, ceramic, or plastic bowl. Discard chokecherry pulp.

Return the juice to the pot. Add the sugar and the fruit pectin. Heat to a full rolling boil and boil hard for one minute.

Remove from heat and pour liquid into hot, sterilized 1-cup sealable bottles.

Seal immediately with paraffin.

Colin Cobb, a freelance writer, writes travel, how-to, and general interest articles in magazines such as *Military Lifestyle Magazine*. Cobb, a cowboy poet, has appeared at gatherings throughout the Southwest and has two chapbooks in print, *A Cowboy Tale* and *Cowboy Cookin'* (WordWright Press). Cobb lives near Las Cruces, New Mexico.

EXCERPT FROM

COWBOY COOKIN'

Bread's the staff of life, you know,
Even the Good Book says it's so!

And I'll tell you what I have always said:
A body has just got to have bread.
That's the way the cowboys all feel.
Without it, a meal just ain't a meal.

Light bread, biscuits, or a sourdough slice,
Cornbread, Dodgers, or frybread, it's all pretty nice.
Gives you something for a gravy sop,
Something with which the meal can top.

Just spread a hunk of bread with butter that's sweet,
Add a smear of jam and you've got a instant treat
So good to eat
That it's right hard to beat.

Published by WordWright Press

Frybread

2 cups flour (or more)　　　　*1 cup warm milk*
2 tablespoons baking powder　*shortening to fry*
1 pinch salt

In a deep bowl, combine the flour, baking powder, and salt. Add milk and mix to make a heavy dough, adding more flour if it looks too wet. Cover dough and set in a warm place to rise.

Divide dough into 4-inch patties, ¼ inch thick. Using a skillet or a deep fryer with hot shortening 1 inch deep, fry the patties, turning once or twice, until the bread is brown and cooked through.

Serve most any old way—dust with sugar, slather with butter, smear with jam, or drench with honey.

D on Coldsmith has written more than thirty books. The bulk of his fiction is in a series of historical novels, the *Spanish Bit Saga* (Bantam/Doubleday), about the Indians of the Great Plains, beginning with the earliest European contact. There are more than six million copies in print, as well as British and German editions. He has been nominated five times for the WWA Spur Award and won the Spur for best original paperback of 1990, *The Changing Wind*. Coldsmith lives in Emporia, Kansas.

EXCERPT FROM

DAUGHTER OF THE EAGLE

Late that night, long after the village was quiet, Running Eagle slipped noiselessly from her parents' lodge. She carried a small but heavy bundle, retrieved from deep behind the lodge lining.

The girl made her way among the neighboring lodges, pausing to quiet a restless horse as she passed. She came to the stream and threaded her way between scattered trees, finally emerging at a still, deep pool some distance upstream. Here she stopped and set her pack on the grass.

For a long time she stood gazing at the starry sky, silently in communion with the world and its sometimes puzzling events.

At last she knelt and opened the rawhide pack. She took out a smooth, fist-sized object and carefully tossed it into the deepest part of the pool. The resounding plunk in the still night produced an echoing plunk from a startled bullfrog in the reeds. A roosting bird fluttered sleepily and the night was quiet again.

Methodically Running Eagle removed the rest of her carefully collected cooking stones from the pack. One at a time, the remaining stones followed the first one in a calculated, almost ritualistic ceremony. It was as if she were cutting the last ties to the life that might have been, that of a woman in her lodge.

She discarded the last stone and stood for a moment, holding the empty rawhide pack. If anyone had been present to observe, he might have noticed that the face of the warrior woman glistened with tears in the shadowy light of the rising moon.

Published by Bantam Doubleday Dell Publishing Group

Running Eagle's Beef Jerky

RECIPE COURTESY OF DON COLDSMITH

4 pounds round steak, 1 inch thick
¼ cup soy sauce
1 tablespoon Worcestershire sauce
¼ teaspoon black pepper
¼ teaspoon garlic powder
¼ teaspoon onion powder
1 tablespoon liquid-smoke flavoring

Trim excess fat from steak and cut in ¼-inch strips.

To make marinade, in a large, deep glass or ceramic bowl, combine remaining ingredients. Dredge steak slices in marinade, coating all slices thoroughly. Cover and refrigerate overnight.

Preheat oven to lowest possible setting, around 120°F.

Drain strips, pat dry, and lay on a cookie sheet that has been sprayed with vegetable oil. (You can also drape the slices across an oven rack that has a coating of oil.)

Bake, with the oven door held open slightly with a wooden spoon or pencil, for 8–12 hours, or until jerky is barely pliable.

A home dehydrator can be used. Follow the directions that accompany the machine.

James A. Crutchfield, a seventh-generation Nashvillian and author of more than twenty-five books, is a master of American history. Crutchfield is a regular contributor to *Muzzleloader*, *Muzzle Blasts* and other monthly magazines. During Nashville's bicentennial, Jim created and wrote a daily television series which ran throughout the city's bicentennial year, and he is now working on a similar project for the state of Tennessee's bicentennial celebration. His nonfiction book *Eyewitness to American History* (Tamarack Books, Inc.) is considered a must for those who maintain a historical research library. Crutchfield lives in Franklin, Tennessee.

⇒•⇐

EYEWITNESS TO AMERICAN HISTORY

The following is a partial list of New York City food prices (1794) taken from the extensive diary of Médéric-Louis-Elie Moreau de St. Méry, a French visitor to the United States during the years 1793–1798.

Milk (which is abundant) costs $\frac{1}{16}$ of a dollar a pint.

Cider cost $\frac{1}{16}$ of a dollar a pint.

A pound of meat $\frac{1}{10}$ of a dollar a pound if one picks it out, $\frac{1}{16}$ of a dollar not selected.

Mutton $\frac{3}{4}$ of a dollar a hindquarter.

Veal is scarce, and cost $\frac{1}{12}$ of a dollar a pound.

Eggs from $\frac{1}{8}$ dollar to $\frac{3}{16}$ for a dozen.

Green beans $\frac{1}{8}$ of a dollar a bushel.

Butter $\frac{3}{16}$ of a dollar the pound or $\frac{1}{4}$ of a dollar.

Vinegar $\frac{1}{16}$ of a dollar the pint.

Lard $\frac{1}{16}$ of a dollar a pound.

French bread $\frac{1}{16}$ of a dollar for 10 American ounces.

Sea bass $\frac{1}{24}$ of a dollar or $\frac{1}{32}$ a pound.

Eels, 2 or 3 for $\frac{1}{16}$ of a dollar.

Four large beets for $\frac{1}{8}$ of a dollar.

A live pig at the rate of $\frac{5}{96}$ of a dollar a pound; a dead one, $\frac{7}{96}$.

Prime hen chickens, $\frac{1}{4}$ of a dollar.

Coffee at retail, $\frac{1}{16}$ of a dollar a pound.

A mill for grinding coffee, $1\frac{1}{8}$ dollars.

A pair of flatirons, $1\frac{3}{4}$ dollars.

Published by Tamarack Books, Inc.

⇒•⇐

Peanut Soup

RECIPE COURTESY OF JAMES A. CRUTCHFIELD

Crutchfield didn't have list prices for peanuts in the material he compiled from Moreau, but they were a common commodity in that time and, no doubt, they were used in all varieties of cooking. This recipe has been in the Crutchfield family for seven generations.

1 tablespoon butter or margarine	½ cup peanut butter, creamy style
½ cup diced onion	dash each of salt and pepper
½ cup diced celery	1 handful peanuts, dry roasted
1 (10-ounce) can celery soup	and crushed
1 ½ cups water	

In a large soup kettle, melt the butter, then sauté onion and celery. Add the celery soup and water. Stir and bring to a low boil. Add peanut butter and continue to stir until the peanut butter has blended into the soup. Add salt and pepper.

Serve hot. Garnish with crushed peanuts.

Chet Cunningham, using several pseudonyms, has published over 250 novels and nonfiction books and has written six feature film scripts. He has published with Dell, Warner, Jove (and Jove Western), Pinnacle, Gold Eagle, Harlequin, Ballantine, Leisure, Signet, Popular Library, Prentice Hall, G. P. Putnam's Sons, Republic of Texas Press, and a saddlebag full of other publishing houses. There's always a dozen or so of his titles on store shelves. Cunningham lives in San Diego, California.

⇒•◇•⇐

EXCERPT FROM

SURVIVAL TRAIL

Kincaid hoisted himself up, grimacing as his right leg took some weight. He took his cane and went down to the rocks twenty feet away in the dry watercourse and started tipping rocks over with his walking stick. Under the third one he found what he hunted, a three-foot-long rattlesnake coiled with its tail rattling out a deadly warning.

With one deft swing of the cane, Kincaid cut the head off the rattler. He grunted, bent over and picked up the still flopping body of the snake and grinned.

"Bet you've never had rattlesnake for lunch, have you, tenderfoot? Let's find some shade and build a fire. I'm getting hungry just thinking about this delicacy."

They went fifty yards east and found a cut bank in the soft desert soil. It offered two feet of shade. Larson built a fire and Kincaid settled down and skinned the snake and took out the meat from along the backbone. He still had his cup. They cooked the rattlesnake meat in the cup with just enough horse blood to keep it from burning.

Ten minutes later, Larson shook his head as he finished eating the last of his portion of the snake meat. "First I'm drinking horse blood to survive. Now I'm eating rattlesnake meat. I'm not sure I believe this."

Published by Robert Hale, London

⇒•◇•⇐

Deep-Fried Rattler

RECIPE COURTESY OF CHET CUNNINGHAM

This makes for an interesting appetizer.

3 cups vegetable oil	*½ teaspoon black pepper*
2 pounds rattlesnake meat, boned	*½ teaspoon garlic powder*
1½ cups flour	*3 eggs, beaten*
½ teaspoon nutmeg	*½ cup cornmeal*

Heat oil in a deep fryer, large skillet, or Dutch oven.

Wash snake meat in cold water, then pat dry.

In a deep bowl combine flour, nutmeg, pepper, and garlic powder. Dredge snake meat in flour mixture. Dip in beaten eggs, then coat with cornmeal.

Fry in hot oil and place on paper towels to drain.

Sharon Cunningham, owner of Dixie Gun Works, is former editorial director of *Pioneer Press* and editor of *The Blackpowder Annual*. She has been publications director for the National Muzzle Loading Rifle Association, edited the monthly publication *Muzzle Blasts* and the first *The Longhunter Society Muzzleloading Big Game Record Book*, and wrote *Dixie Gun Works' Best of Southern Recipes* (Pioneer Press). Cunningham lives in Union City, Tennessee.

<hr />

EXCERPT FROM

DIXIE GUN WORKS' BEST OF SOUTHERN RECIPES

Here in the northwest corner of Tennessee, we are blessed with a natural phenomenon known worldwide as Reelfoot Lake. It was formed in 1811–1812 during the New Madrid earthquake, when the world was sent askew for four long months. "The Lake" is famous for its duck and goose hunting, and the folks who live in the communities around Reelfoot have always utilized its resources to supplement their livings. My family was one of these, and my mom, Lou (Louise), learned early how to cook duck and geese. As with most Southern cooks, she experimented often; here is one of her wonderful recipes for wild duck (or goose, if you please). This was always the Fowlers' Christmas dinner, courtesy of either Dad or brother, Mike, who were very good at supplying this annual feast.

Published by Pioneer Press

<hr />

Lou's Duck & Wild Rice

RECIPE BY SHARON CUNNINGHAM, AS HANDED DOWN TO HER
BY HER MOTHER, LOU

2 wild ducks, plucked and cleaned
3 quarts salt water (⅓ cup salt to 3 quarts water)
1 cup long-grain and wild rice
2 apples, quartered, then diced, with 1 quarter set aside
2 oranges, quartered, then diced, with 1 quarter set aside
1 package fresh cranberries, chopped
½ cup sliced almonds
salt and pepper to taste
½ teaspoon parsley, plus some for garnish
butter for basting

Soak ducks in salt water for several hours.

To prepare wild rice stuffing, cook rice according to package directions, drain, and combine with the diced apples and oranges, cranberries, almonds, salt and pepper, and ½ teaspoon parsley.

Preheat oven to 300°F.

Remove ducks from salt water, rinse, pat dry with paper towels, and stuff with remaining apple and orange.

Place in a large, shallow baking pan. Brush tops of ducks with butter, cover with a foil tent and roast for 3 hours, basting often with cooking juices.

Remove from oven, remove apple/orange quarters, and fill body cavities with wild rice stuffing. Baste duck with butter and cooking juices and return it, uncovered, to the oven to brown, for 20–25 minutes.

Andrew Dequasie is the author of two novels, including *Thirsty*, a humorous western set in an Idaho gold-mining town. *Thirsty* won the Western Writers of America Medicine Pipe Bearer's Award. Dequasie is also the author of several short stories including "A Hundred Pounds of Gold" featured in *New Frontiers II*. In addition he has written for periodicals and chemical journals. Dequasie lives in Pownal, Vermont.

EXCERPT FROM

THIRSTY

The following recipe and excerpt copy appears in Chapter 6, "The Venison Feast." The range cook named Frypan has carelessly bragged that he could serve up the world's best venison feast at $3.00 per head. Even more carelessly, he accepts droves of customers before he finds that deer are mighty scarce in the region. Doc Crane tells him that jackrabbit cooked in a pressure cooker and heavily spiced might pass for venison. They find an 80-gallon boiler and manage to bag one deer and enough jackrabbits to serve the customers, who are never to know it wasn't all venison.

Suddenly, a hiss of steam erupted from the boiler. Doc looked at it and jumped to his feet. "Who in hell piled all those bricks on the pressure control?"

"We need the pressure, Doc; that stuff has got to cook!" Frypan said.

"Douse the fire! Douse the fire!" Doc shouted, frantically looking for water.

Then, with a mighty WHOOMP, a piece of leather gasket blew out from under the lid and a cloud of steam belched into the room. "Duck!" Doc shouted, dropping flat on the dirt along with Frypan, George, and Downwind.

"Do you reckon it's done?" Frypan asked when the steam had cleared a bit.

"Oh, it's done, all right," Doc answered.

Published by Walker and Company

Faux Venison

One deer
As many jackrabbits as four skilled hunters can bag in one day
All the vegetables in season
All the spices in town

Load an 80-gallon pressure cooker with all the above and with ample water.
    Cook until the lid gasket blows out.
    De-bone and dice the meat.
    Hide the jackrabbit bones.
    Leave the deer bones in sight.
    Serve free whiskey before the feast.
    Serve the venison to the few who are sober.
    Serve the jackrabbit to the rest.

J ohn Duncklee is the author of *Coyotes I Have Known* and *Good Year for the Buzzards*, both published by the University of Arizona Press. In addition, he has published short stories for *Raconteur, High Country,* and *Western Pocket,* and articles for many publications including *Arizona Highways, Tucson Lifestyle, Cowboy, The Tombstone Epitaph, Christian Science Monitor, Sierra Club Books* and *Defenders of Wildlife International.* He writes a monthly column, "The View From the Porch," for local papers. Many of his works have been published in Spanish. His latest novel, *Quest for the The Eagle Feather,* for middle readers, was published by Northland Publishing. Duncklee, and his wife Penny, spend their winters in Oracle, Arizona, and their summers in Alpine, Arizona.

EXCERPT FROM

THE VIEW FROM THE PORCH

When living in southern Arizona what quickly gets added to your vocabulary is *chubasco*. Chubascos are Mexico's West Coast hurricanes that have been known to ravage towns and cities along the coast of the Golfo de California, The Vermillion Sea, or the Sea of Cortez, whatever name of the Gulf of California you want to use. . . .

I remember experiencing a chubasco quite a number of years ago. The Hotel Miramar near Guaymas was operating in its heyday. There was a group of us, mostly engaged in buying Mexican steers, sitting in the lounge discussing the closing of the border to cattle exports.

Word had gotten around about the predicted arrival of a chubasco, but rarely did anything happen like that serve to clear the lounge at the Miramar. . . .

Our waiter had brought a large platter of botana, a custom in the land of jalapeños and tequila. Since Guaymas is famous for its shrimp, there was a generous amount of these crustaceans on the platter.

The rain began to accompany the wind, and noisily splattered the glass of the large windows in the lounge. Soon the huge drops hitting the glass with a staccato rattle brought one of the fellows to his feet for a look at the storm. He weaved over to the nearest window, peered out at the storm, and as he returned to the table he wore an incredulous, wide-eyed, expression on his face. "Hey you guys. You have to go look out the window. It's rainin' shrimp!"

Most of us obliged our companion and went to the window. As we were scrutinizing the storm one fellow focused his attention to the spacious lawn beyond the well-pruned shrubery. "If it's rainin' shrimp," he slurred. "How come there's no shrimp on the grass?"

Things have changed in Mexico since then. The Hotel Miramar burned down. The shrimp boats have over-fished the Gulf, but the chubascos still persist. Should you be in some coastal resort bar during one of those hurricanes and look out the window, you probably won't see it rainin' shrimp. Of course, that might depend on how many margaritas you have consumed while waiting out the storm.

Published by The Connection *(Arivaca, Arizona)*

Camarones Borrachos (Drunken Shrimp)

RECIPE COURTESY OF JOHN DUNCKLEE

This is a very easy appetizer to make, and it is a hit at friendly gatherings. Use only the best tequila and don't forget to have a bracer or two for yourself. Mescal may be used in place of tequila. CAUTION! If mescal is used, insure the worm does not come in contact with the shrimp because this causes terrible hangovers in shrimp. Hungover shrimp are likely to stick to the pan.

4 cups water
1 pound shrimp, medium size
3 tablespoons butter
1 tablespoon chili powder
  (your choice of heat—I use mild)

2 tablespoons salsa
1 cup tequila
4 limes, quartered

Bring the water to a brisk boil. Blanche shrimp until they just start to turn pink. Remove from heat and rinse immediately in cold water; peel and de-vein.

  Melt butter in a deep skillet. Add chili powder and salsa, and bring to a simmer. Add shrimp and coat thoroughly with salsa mixture. Add tequila and simmer for 20 seconds; turn shrimp and simmer for 30 more seconds. Serve with limes.

Loren D. Estleman, the recipient of two Spur Awards and three Shamus Awards (from Private Eye Writers of America), is the author of *The Wister Trace*, a work of criticism on classic Western novels. His historical Westerns *This Old Bill* and *Bloody Season* were nominated for the Pulitzer, and *The High Rocks* received an American Book Award nomination. One of his recent westerns, *City of Widows*, is considered a flawless Western. Estleman lives in Michigan with his wife, Debi, who is also a writer.

≡>◇<≡

EXCERPT FROM

CITY OF WIDOWS

As a cook, Dolores del Guerrero was Mexico's best-kept secret. Her tortillas were thin enough to read a newspaper through, yet strong enough to hoist a plateful of chili pepper without crumbling, and they melted on contact with the human tongue. The wine was blood-red and strong, poured by Jesus from a green bottle whose label bore the Diamond Horn crest. All the food was served by the woman. Axtaca, who on the trail would have out-starved a Spartan, filled his glass when the rest of us had had enough. Francisco and Carlos were absent, probably sharing a table with the others in the bunkhouse.

Published by Forge

≡>◇<≡

Tortilla Soup

RECIPE COURTESY OF LOREN D. ESTLEMAN

Chiles pasilla (sometimes called chile ancho) is packaged in dry form and available at most Latin markets or in the international section of supermarkets.

6 corn tortillas
½ cup olive oil
¼ cup minced white onion
1 clove garlic, minced
2 cups tomatoes, chopped
3 cups chicken stock

¼ teaspoon cumin
salt to taste
1 cup feta cheese, crumbled
3 chiles pasilla, seeded and chopped
¼ cup chopped cilantro

Preheat oven to 200°F.

Cut the tortillas into thin strips. Spread the tortilla strips on a cookie sheet and bake for 10 minutes. With a spatula, turn the strips and let bake for another 5 minutes or until they are firm enough to break. Remove strips from oven and let cool.

In a deep skillet heat the olive oil. Fry the tortilla strips until lightly browned. With a slotted spoon remove the strips to drain. Sauté the onion and garlic until the onion is translucent. Add the tomatoes and stir constantly until the mixture thickens. Add the chicken stock and cumin.

Cover and simmer for 20 minutes. Strain the liquid into a pot, squeezing some of the onion mixture through the strainer into the soup. Salt to taste. Keep the soup hot.

Line the bottom of warmed soup bowls with the tortilla strips.

Ladle the soup into the bowls and sprinkle with feta cheese, chiles pasilla, and cilantro.

Serve hot.

LOREN D. ESTLEMAN   ❖ 49 ❖

Jim Marion Etter, a freelance writer, writes Western fiction and nonfiction, and is a noted storyteller. Among his nonfiction works is *Ghost-Town Tales of Oklahoma* (New Forums Press). Etter lives in Oklahoma City, Oklahoma.

EXCERPT FROM

GHOST-TOWN TALES OF OKLAHOMA

It was even more exciting than their big event every year, the big May Day Picnic down near Doan's Crossing—the place where, Naomi was told, she was born. The once-a-year picnic was where everybody she had ever known—the people from where her family used to live on the south side of the river and people on this side where they lived now—went and laughed and had fun and ate from an enormous pile of delicious food put together by the many families.

Her mother, in fact, always seemed to take enough to feed everyone there. She'd fix plenty of fried chicken, black-eyed peas, fried okra and nearly every kind of good eats one could imagine and pack it all in washtubs that would be loaded into the wagon—which normally they all would ride across the river.

Published by New Forums Press

Oklahoma-Style Fried Okra

RECIPE COURTESY OF JIM MARION ETTER

1 pound fresh okra
  (40–50 three-inch pods)
½ cup flour
½ cup cornmeal
½ teaspoon salt
¼ teaspoon hot chili powder

¼ teaspoon cumin
¼ teaspoon white pepper
2 eggs, whipped
3 tablespoons evaporated milk
2 cups vegetable oil
3 cloves garlic, mashed

Wash okra and remove stems and tips. Cut okra in halves and set aside.

In a deep bowl, combine flour, cornmeal, salt, chili powder, cumin, and pepper, and blend thoroughly.

In a small bowl, beat eggs and milk together.

Dip okra into milk mixture, then into cornmeal mixture to coat. Set aside until all the okra is coated.

Preheat oven to 250°F.

Heat a deep skillet until a drop of water quickly sizzles away. Add vegetable oil and mashed garlic. Sauté garlic until it starts to brown, then discard garlic.

Fry a handful of okra at a time, making sure to keep pieces separate so they don't lump together.

Remove with a slotted spoon to a paper towel to drain.

Keep warm in the preheated oven while frying the remaining okra.

E lizabeth Fackler has published seven novels concerning the legacy of the West. Among these are *Billy the Kid: The Legend of El Chivato*. Her newest novel, *Badlands*, came out in late 1996. Fackler lives in Tombstone, Arizona.

BILLY THE KID: THE LEGEND OF EL CHIVATO

Celsa was slapping out tortillas for his meal when he came in. He gave her a kiss on the cheek then sat down on the settee to read the newspaper. Her hands made quiet sounds shaping the tortillas, pat, pat, pat, flattening the round balls of dough, laying them on the griddle where they hissed as they rose and puffed, then fell just before she flipped them with her fingertips. Pat, pat, pat, the dough for the next one, the singe of the heat again, and pat, pat, pat. The sound was somnolent, the fragrance enticing.

When she lifted the lid off the pot of beans to stir them, the fragrance of chile mingled with the toasting bread, and the Kid sat up. "What else you got to eat, Celsa?"

"Beans," she said with a shrug. "When Saval comes home, we will have money again."

"Pete butchered a steer today. Think I'll walk over and cut me a steak."

"Okay," she answered with a smile. "I will cook it for you."

"Thanks," he said, walking out as he was, in his stocking feet and shirt-sleeves, without his gun.

Published by Forge/St. Martin's Press, Inc.

Celsa's Chile Beans

RECIPE COURTESY OF ELIZABETH FACKLER

1 pound pinto or
   Anasazi beans
4 cups water
½ teaspoon salt
4 cups beef broth
3 cloves garlic, minced
1 cup chopped white onion
¼ teaspoon oregano

¼ teaspoon marjoram
¼ teaspoon cumin
1 bay leaf
¼ cup chili powder
1 cup diced green chiles
sour cream and cilantro
   for garnish

Sort beans, rinse, and add to a deep pot or Dutch oven. Add the water and salt and bring to a brisk boil. Reduce to a simmer, cover, and cook for one hour; add water if needed.

Add beef broth, garlic, onion, oregano, marjoram, cumin, bay leaf, and chili powder. Cover and cook until beans are tender, about 2 hours.

Add green chiles, cover, and cook for 20 more minutes.

Serve with a dash of sour cream sprinkled with cilantro.

Phyllis de la Garza is the author of three published books, including *Chaco, The Story of Dos Cabezas,* and *The Apache Kid* (1995 WWA Spur finalist). De la Garza lives in Willcox, Arizona.

EXCERPT FROM

CHACO

Doña Eugenia was fixing supper in the yard, beside a fire. Her gray hair was parted and drawn back into two thin braids. Her once pretty face was deeply lined from years of sun, wind, and hard work. She wore a clean pink apron over her cotton dress.

"You're late," she said. "I hope you brought enough firewood."

Don Magdaleno dropped the bundle next to her, and she untied the rope. A nosy chicken came to inspect the wood. Don Magdaleno studied the bird. "This hen will soon be ready for the pot."

Doña Eugenia added wood to the fire. "When these nopales are ready, we can eat." She nodded at a dish of prickly pear cactus leaves she'd gathered earlier in the day. Now, she used a knife to slice off the thorns. Then, she cut each leaf into small squares and mixed them with chiles, onions, and tomatoes. Finally, she poured it all into some hot fat in an iron skillet. It sizzled. Spicy aroma filled the air.

Wearily, Don Magdaleno sat on the ground near the fire. He liked the smell of frying cactus. "The walk was long today. What's new around here?"

Published by New Readers Press

—≫•≪—

Stuffed Prickly Pear Leaves,
page 56

Stuffed Prickly Pear Leaves

RECIPE COURTESY OF PHYLLIS DE LA GARZA

Prickly pear leaves, or nopales, as they are called in the Southwest, can be purchased at most international or Latin markets. Commercial nopales are usually de-thorned. Nopales can also be picked fresh in the spring and de-thorned with a sharp knife.

8 fresh prickly pear leaves,
  3–5 inches long
3-4 cups water
¼ teaspoon baking soda
1 small onion, chopped
¼ teaspoon salt
¾ cup all-purpose flour
6 egg whites

pepper to taste
1 cup lard
4 thick slices white cheese
  (preferably queso asadero)
½ teaspoon mild chili powder
1 clove garlic, minced
4 scallions, chopped
1 cup beef stock

Clean the prickly pear leaves (nopales) in cold water, making sure to remove any hidden thorns. In a large stew pot bring water to a boil.

Add nopales, baking soda, onion, and salt.

Reduce to a simmer and cook, uncovered, for 45 minutes or until tender, adding water as needed.

Drain and rinse in cold water. Pat leaves dry.

In a mixing bowl, combine ½ cup of the flour, egg whites, salt, and pepper to form a batter. Dust leaves with remaining ¼ cup of flour.

Melt lard in frying pan.

Place cheese slices between two leaves, then dredge leaves in the batter. Fry leaves in the lard and remove. Cover leaves with foil to keep warm.

Repeat process until all leaves have been fried.

Pour off all but about 1 tablespoon of the lard, leaving the dregs in the skillet. To the skillet add chile powder, garlic, scallions, and fry for about two minutes. Add beef stock and cook over medium heat until sauce starts to thicken. (For hotter sauce, add cayenne, or habañero salsa, or your preference of hot sauce.)

Add fried nopales and cook for two more minutes.

Serve hot with the sauce.

Kathleen O'Neal Gear comes to the writing trade with a background in archaeology, history, and Native American studies. Gear has authored or co-authored several novels including *This Widowed Land, Sand in the Wind,* and *Thin Moon and Cold Mist,* all published by TOR. In addition, Gear is co-author with her husband W. Michael Gear of *The First North Americans* series: *People of the Wolf, People of the Fire, People of the Earth, People of the River, People of the Sea, People of the Lakes, People of the Lightning,* and *People of the Silence.* She and her husband live on an isolated ranch in northwestern Wyoming with a small herd of buffalo and a Shetland sheepdog. Their home sits at the edge of the Wind River Indian Reservation.

EXCERPT FROM

THIN MOON AND COLD MIST

Tears glinted in Jeremy's eyes.

Macey smiled sympathetically. "You all right, Jeremy?" When he squeezed her hand back, she hesitated, then said, "You know what? I been thinking about baking up a wild rice pie. Does that sound good to you?"

Jeremy sniffed and wiped at his clogged nose. "I never heard of such a thing. What is it?"

"Oh, landsakes, honey! Wild rice pie's about the best eatin' this side of paradise. You beat up three eggs, pour in four ounces of maple sugar and six ounces of molasses, then blend in 12 ounces of cooked wild rice, pour it all into a pie crust and bake her good 'til she sets up. Usually 'bout forty-five minutes. Want to try it?"

"Yes, Macey. I'd like to."

"Good," she said, standing up. "Come on. We'll start making the crust."

Published by Forge

Wild Rice Pie

RECIPE COURTESY OF KATHLEEN O'NEAL GEAR

3 eggs, beaten
4 ounces maple sugar or turbinado (raw sugar)
6 ounces molasses
12 ounces wild rice, cooked
1 (9-inch) pie crust, frozen

Preheat oven to 375°F.

In a large mixing bowl, combine eggs, sugar, and molasses; blend thoroughly. Add wild rice and mix well. Pour the mixture into an uncooked pie crust.

Bake for 40–45 minutes, or until the pie sets.

Author W. Michael Gear is known for the bestselling First North Americans fiction series he co-authors with his wife, Kathleen O'Neal Gear. His other credits include *Wolf Dream, Big Horn Legacy, Long Ride Home,* and *The Morning River*. A trained physical anthropologist and an expert on the American Frontier, Gear debunks many myths about our American heritage as he portrays the people and the spirit of early America with rich detail and authenticity. Gear lives near Thermopolis, Wyoming.

EXCERPT FROM

LONG RIDE HOME

When the animals had moved as close as they would get, Theo shot an old cow. As she fell, a younger cow walked up to sniff the body. When she turned sideways, Theo shot her. In a like manner he killed another two animals before rising to his feet and sauntering back to his horse. The buffalo continued to drift past the dead.

At Theo's wave, Dolly and Henry drove the wagon up to the bodies. Theo had retrieved his horse and started skinning the animals.

"You only shot four!" Henry cried, watching the herd move off. "You could'a kilt a hunert!"

"Henry," Theo said woodenly, "get off your duff and get down here. You're gonna see once and for all just what you got yourself into!"

Wild Rice Pie

By dark they had skinned the four animals and staked the hides out. Henry collapsed by the fire. He didn't even eat, but fell soundly asleep on the spot. Theo, under no such compulsion, ate heartily of hump roast and slightly cooked liver. Dolly cringed when he poured bile over the bloody stuff.

Published by Forge

Roast Buffalo Hump

RECIPE COURTESY OF W. MICHAEL GEAR

A large sirloin roast or de-boned rib eye roast can be used if buffalo is not available. Buffalo can be ordered at most supermarkets or from specialty butcher shops.

1 teaspoon lemon-pepper seasoning	*¼ cup apple-cider vinegar*
	4–5 pound buffalo roast
1 teaspoon ground sage	*3 tablespoons olive oil*
¼ teaspoon garlic powder	*½ cup tomato juice*
2 tablespoons lemon juice	*1 cup beef broth*
1 cup red wine	*3 tablespoons flour*

To make marinade, in a deep, ceramic or glass bowl, combine lemon-pepper seasoning, ground sage, garlic powder, lemon juice, red wine, and cider vinegar. Add buffalo roast and marinate, in the refrigerator, for 6 hours, turning every hour.

Preheat oven to 350°F.

In a deep roasting pan, add the olive oil and bring to moderate heat. Braise the roast on all sides. Add the marinade and tomato juice. Insert a meat thermometer and bake for 20 minutes per pound or until the thermometer reads 140°F (slightly rare), or 160°F (medium). Baste frequently. To avoid tough meat, never roast buffalo above 160°F degrees.

To make gravy, in a skillet combine ½ cup of the roasting pan juices with the beef broth and the flour. Bring to a slow boil, then to a simmer, stirring constantly. Reduce to a slightly thick gravy and serve over slices of the buffalo roast.

Robin Gibson has published four Western novels in his Whiskey City Series (Avalon Books). Among these are *The Sheriff of Whiskey City*, *The Bandits of Whiskey City*, *The Legend of Whiskey City*, and *The Doctor of Whiskey City*. In addition, Avalon has published his other Western, *Riders of Black Dawn*. A seasonal traveler, Gibson spends his time in Walsh, Colorado, and Tucson, Arizona.

⇒◆⇐

EXCERPT FROM

THE DOCTOR OF WHISKEY CITY

Her cheeks turning pink, Eddy hung her head. "I never cooked a pot of beans that big before. I didn't realize it would take so much longer to get them done."

Seeing the hurt look that sprang to Eddy's face, I was sorely tempted to smack Turley, but since I couldn't reach him, I had to settle for shooting him a dark scowl. "Just shut up and eat. They ain't gonna hurt you none."

Turley hooted, slapping the table. "Now, I don't know about that. Why, a man could chip a tooth on these things," he said, banging the table again. "I bet I could load them up in my shotgun and bag a buffalo."

Published by Avalon Books

⇒◆⇐

Cave Man Beans

RECIPE COURTESY OF ROBIN GIBSON

Don't let the story line fool you. Gibson's Cave Man Beans are a tasty treat.

2 pounds pinto beans, sorted and rinsed	2 tablespoons apple-cider vinegar
8 cups water	½ cup brown sugar (or 3 tablespoons molasses)
1 (16-ounce) can chopped tomatoes	1 cup catsup
1 tablespoon dry mustard	1 green bell pepper, chopped

Soak the beans overnight in the water.

Bring the beans and water to a boil, then reduce to a simmer; cover and cook for 45 minutes.

Preheat oven to 350°F.

In a deep casserole dish combine beans and broth with remaining ingredients and bake, covered, for 2½ hours.

Remove cover and bake for 30 more minutes.

Charles Hackenberry's second book, *I Rode with Jesse James* (HarperCollins) was published in 1996. His first novel, *Friends,* won a Spur award as the Best Western Novel of 1993. When not at his word processor spinning yarns, Dr. Hackeberry teaches American literature and technical writing at the Altoona campus of Penn State University. He and his wife, Barbara, live in the Bald Eagle Valley of Pennsylvania with their surrogate grandchild (a Jack Russell Terrier) named Bobby.

⇒•⇐

EXCERPT FROM

I RODE WITH JESSE JAMES

Ma turned around to face me in the doorway. "Just how many chances do you think a man that's been in prison is going to get, anyway? A chance to make something of hisself?"

I was going to give her an answer of some kind, but she barged ahead and gave me no chance. "I did all right before you got out of jail, after your daddy died, and I can do it again. Bill Hudspeth can do the plowing and the heavy chores."

She went into the kitchen, leaving me there sitting at the table, scratching my jaw and trying to figure out what in the hell was going on. I was still chewing on it when she put a big wedge of milk pie down in front of me. I didn't even know she'd baked it. Still warm from the oven and me not even smelled it when I come in from the field.

Milk pie, my favorite. She must of stirred it up right after she read my Pinkerton letter. But I still wasn't sure she really wanted me to go or if she just wanted me to be free to go if I wanted to.

Published by HarperCollins

⇒•⇐

Milk Pie

RECIPE COURTESY OF CHARLES HACKENBERRY

1 pie shell, unbaked
½ cup brown sugar
¼ cup flour
dash salt

2 tablespoons butter or margarine
2 cups fresh milk (skim is a
   good substitute)

Preheat oven to 375°F.

Over the bottom of the unbaked pie shell, crumble the brown sugar. Sprinkle the flour over the sugar and shake in the salt. Dot with butter. Slowly pour in the milk.

Bake for 30 minutes.

That's it! Easy and quick. For a variation, you can add a handful or two of blackberries, dewberries, mulberries, or huckleberries—black raspberries are my favorite. A few crumbled walnuts or pecans sprinkled in give this rather flat pie a little height. It eats a whole lot better than it writes.

Stella Hughes, a cowhand in her own right, is the author of *Hashknife Cowboy: Recollections of Mack Hughes* and *Chuck Wagon Cookin'*, both published by the University of Arizona Press. In addition, Hughes writes a monthly column, "Bacon an' Beans," for *Western Horseman Magazine*. Hughes lives on the Eagle Creek Ranch somewhere out from Clifton, Arizona.

⟹◆⟸

EXCERPT FROM

CHUCK WAGON COOKIN'

DEE-ZERTS

They wake in the mornin' 'fore the break of day
Send you on a circle twenty miles away
The grub is bread and beans, and coffee black as ink
An' water so full of alkali, it ain't fit to drink.

    Cowboys, in the early days, had an insatiable craving for sweets. It was no doubt due to the fact they so seldom got to town to stow up on candy or bakery goods. Also, many ranch cooks lacked skills in making desserts, such as pies and cakes—or did not have the proper ingredients. In any event, a good cook that made plenty of puddings, cobblers, cakes, pies, doughnuts or cookies was apt to be considered indispensable on any outfit. A cook talented in this line, even if he be the most evil-tempered man alive, was considered better than an easy-going cook that seldom, if ever, turned out a tallow pudding or made doughnuts or cookies. An amiable cook—one so lax he would allow the cowboys to line up at the ovens with their leggin's floppin' in the dust—or one who kept a hot pot of coffee ready twenty-four hours a day—or condoned raiding his chuck box between meals—might be considered a marvel. But, unless he was forever making some sweet concoction, labeled "dee-zert," he could never become the cowboy's favorite.

Published by University of Arizona Press

⟹◆⟸

Vinegar Cobbler

RECIPE COURTESY OF STELLA HUGHES

Hughes claims this recipe came from the collection of Bessie Filleman, Four Bar Ranch, near Eagle Creek, Clifton, Arizona, circa 1923.

4 cups sugar	*¼ pound butter*
2 ½ cups water	*nutmeg to taste*
¾ cup vinegar	*1 unbaked pie dough*

Combine all ingredients, except the pie dough, in a large skillet or Dutch oven. Over medium heat, bring mixture to a rolling boil, then reduce to a simmer. Cook until thickened, about 10–15 minutes.

Roll out pie dough until it's thin, then cut into strips about ½-inch wide. Preheat oven to 350°F.

Crisscross the top of the cobbler mixture with the pie-dough strips.

Bake for 15–20 minutes or until the crust is a golden brown.

If the pie seems thin, that's the way it should be. This is not a custard-style dessert and is best baked in a Dutch oven at a campsite.

Sharon Ihle has authored several historical-romance novels including *Wild Rose, The Law and Miss Penny, Marrying Miss Shylo, Wildcat,* and *The Bride Wore Spurs.* Ihle lives in El Cajon, California.

EXCERPT FROM

THE BRIDE WORE SPURS

The table was laden with platters of ham, pork fillets, Donegal pie, and broth.

". . . And so Lord," Kate prayed over the meal, "may the blessing of the five loaves and two fishes be ours, and may the King who made division put a good heart to the babe who's coming our way."

Hawke and Lacey exchanged a meaningful glance, while Caleb just sat there staring at his empty supper plate. Finally he raised his head and looked at his wife. "What's all this chatter about babes and children?"

Hawke put the news in ranching terms. "What she said was that she'd be calving sometime in March, and you're the herd bull responsible for the new breed of Weatherspoon."

Caleb blanched, which was saying something since the summer sun had baked his skin until it was almost as dark as Hawke's. "Calving? You mean . . . Kate is . . ."

"Aye, you silly fool," said the mother-to-be. "I think I shall be, er, *calving,* sometime around the end of March."

And just like that, the big former mountain man passed out. Then he pitched forward across the table, his bulbous nose digging a mighty deep post hole in Kate's Donegal pie.

Published by Harper Paperbacks

Kate's Donegal Pie,
page 68

Kate's Donegal Pie

RECIPE COURTESY OF SHARON IHLE

3 cups mashed potatoes
3 scallions, minced
¼ teaspoon black pepper
½ teaspoon sage
3 hard-boiled eggs,
  sliced ¼-inch thick

½ pound bacon, fried crisp
¼ cup butter, melted
2 (9-inch) unbaked pie crusts
1 raw egg
1 tablespoon milk

Preheat oven to 350°F.

In a mixing bowl combine mashed potatoes, scallions, black pepper, and sage; mix well.

Spoon potato mixture into one of the unbaked pie crusts, mounding to the center. Arrange egg slices over potatoes, then add bacon strips. Pour melted butter over all.

Cover with the other pie crust and seal edges.

In a small dish combine raw egg and milk. Brush egg and milk mixture on pie crust, then poke several holes in the crust.

Bake for 1 hour or until the pie crust is golden brown.

J ohn Jakes sold his first story when he was nineteen and his first book a year later. In 1970, after seventeen years in the advertising business, he turned to writing full time. Today, Jakes is best known as a historical novelist. His eight-volume American Bicentennial Series, *The Kent Family Chronicles,* has sold over 40 million copies, and his trilogy, *North and South, Love and War,* and *Heaven and Hell* have likewise been bestsellers. Since then he has written two other bestsellers, *California Gold* and *Homeland.*

EXCERPT FROM

CALIFORNIA GOLD

"Ladies and gentlemen, welcome to my house and this celebration of the new century. I was not born in this state, but I am now a Californian to the bone." Some applause and murmurs greeted that: guests had been plied with unlimited amounts of Cresta Blanca champagne, the state's finest, before the banquet.

"Therefore, the dinner you're about to enjoy is a California dinner. Every dish is native to the state. You will be given a printed menu in a moment. Meanwhile, I hope you'll look with special favor on the stuffing and the glaze of the caille roti—native quail from the San Joaquin. Cooking is a love of mine, and I prepared both the stuffing and the glaze. I confess I've never cooked for a hundred people before. That's a mighty long time in the kitchen."

"The wines, too, are Californian. Tonight we celebrate not only the New Year, and the twentieth century, but the state we love."

He lifted his brimming glass.

"To California. And your very good health."

Published by Ballantine Books

———◆———

Stuffed Roasted Cornish Game Hen

RECIPE COURTESY OF JOHN JAKES

Quail is the preferred fowl for this recipe, but quail are not always available, so I've substituted the more common Cornish game hens. Should you have quail available, suggested serving is two per person.

4 Cornish game hens
generous pinch each of garlic
  powder, marjoram, ground
  ginger, salt, and pepper
2 tablespoons butter, melted over
  low heat
1 cup brown rice, cooked
¼ cup piñons (pine nuts),
  chopped coarse
¼ cup coarsely chopped
  black walnuts

4 dried apricots, minced
1 red bell pepper, minced
1 green bell pepper, minced
1 cup orange juice
1 cup chardonnay
4 shallots, minced
½ teaspoon dry mustard
minced chives and chopped black
  olives for garnish

Clean game hens in cold water and pat dry.

Combine garlic powder, marjoram, ginger, salt, and pepper in a mortar; grind and mix. Rub spice mixture over the game hens. In a pan over medium heat, add melted butter. Brown the birds, breast-side down. Remove the birds from the pan and set them aside. Reserve drippings.

Preheat oven to 325°F.

In a mixing bowl combine brown rice, piñons, walnuts, apricots, red and green bell pepper, and drippings from the pan. Mix thoroughly. Stuff each bird tightly with the rice/nut mixture.

In a sealable, 3-quart casserole dish add the orange juice, chardonnay, shallots, and dry mustard. Whisk to blend ingredients. Place birds, breast-side up, in the casserole dish. Cover. Seal remaining stuffing in an aluminum pouch and place in the oven with the game hens.

Bake for 25 minutes.

Remove cover from casserole and bake for 10 more minutes.

Remove birds and stuffing to a large plate and cover with foil to keep warm.

De-glaze cooking liquid in casserole dish, then pour into a saucepan and, over medium heat, reduce by one-third or until sauce starts to thicken.

Serve the game hens with the orange/wine sauce, and stuffing on the side.

Stuffed Roast Cornish Game Hen

Author W. C. Jameson has written over twenty books, including *Tales of the Guadalupe Mountains* (Republic of Texas Press), and from August House Publishing Company, *Buried Treasures of the Southwest, Buried Treasures of the Ozarks and Appalachians, Buried Treasures of the Rocky Mountains, Buried Treasures of Texas,* and others. In addition, Jameson has seen into print *The Guadalupe Mountain: Island in the Desert* (Texas Western Press) as well as over two hundred magazine articles and a thousand newspaper columns in publications including *The Log Cabin Democrat.* Several of his works are audio releases. Jameson lives in Conway, Arkansas.

⟫⟩◦⟨⟪

EXCERPT FROM

A MAN MUST HAVE HIS MEAT

Shortly before sundown the single-engine plane landed at the tiny Wyoming airport where I was greeted by my hosts and several of their friends. After I was introduced all around, one of the greeters, a grandmotherly type, examined my lean, denim-clad frame and exclaimed, "My goodness! Let's get this poor starved thing into town and feed him some meat."

I pondered her comment for weeks afterward and am still not certain what she meant, but I think the well-intentioned lady believed Texans are forced to go meatless for long stretches of time.

That evening, I was provided a slice of beef large enough to sustain four husky lumberjacks. Each evening thereafter, beef was the main course at dinner—large, tasty, juicy, sizzling steaks, briskets, and prime rib. Food yuppies and health fanatics would have passed out cold from thoughts of cholesterol overdose. I was told there are no yuppies in Wyoming.

Throughout the week, the friendly Wyomingites caused me to think deeply about the role of meat in society. I realized that our ages-old obsession with meat has long passed into the language and cultural fabric via a number of proverbial, metaphorical, and even religious avenues.

In the Bible, for instance, Cain killed Abel over his brother's gift, not of potatoes or broccoli, but of meat. When the prodigal son returned, did the father send out for a salad? No, he ordered a fatted calf.

One Christian denomination tried for generations to ban meat on Fridays, but the rule didn't stick.

The very word "meat," in fact, has traditionally stood for all food. The first definition of meat listed in the *Oxford English Dictionary* reads, "Food in general; anything used as nourishment for men and animals."

Like it or not, America is meat country, and beef rises head and shoulders above all the other kinds.

A man must have his meat!

Published by The Log Cabin Democrat

⟫⟩◦⟨⟪

Texas Brisket

RECIPE COURTESY OF W. C. JAMESON

For optimum flavor, the brisket must have a bit of fat on it. The cholesterol-conscious are free to remove the fat, but they do so at great sacrifice to taste. The special barbecue flavor of a brisket cooked on an open grill is obtained during the first 30 to 45 minutes of exposure to the coals. It's common for mesquite chips to leave the brisket with a rich, dark brown crust.

4–6 cups mesquite or hickory chips	*¼ teaspoon cumin*
½ teaspoon ground black pepper	*¼ teaspoon red (or cayenne) pepper*
½ teaspoon garlic powder	*1 (3–4 pound) beef brisket*
½ teaspoon onion powder	

At least one hour before grilling, soak the wood chips in enough water to cover. In a barbecue grill add enough charcoal to cover bottom about two briquets deep. Light the charcoal and let the coals go to gray while you prepare the brisket. Combine the black pepper, garlic powder, onion powder, cumin, and red pepper in a mortar or spice bowl. Grind with a pestle (or the back of a heavy spoon) to release the spice oils and to blend the spices.

Wash the brisket under cold water, then pat dry with a towel. Place the brisket on a cutting surface or counter top and coat the meat evenly with the spice mixture. Set meat aside to absorb the spices.

When the coals have burned down to a medium heat, toss in a couple handfuls of chips. Lay the rubbed brisket on the grill; close the grill lid or cover with foil and cook for about 45 minutes, turning it every ten minutes or so. Add wood chips as needed.

Ten minutes before removing brisket from grill, preheat oven to 200°F.

When the meat has a rich, dark brown crust, remove it from the grill and set it in a roasting pan. Cover with heavy aluminum foil and place in the oven.

Cook for 1 hour per pound of meat.

The result is a succulent, tender slab of beef, rich in taste and as tender as veal. (Don't salt the meat until after it has been cooked, or it won't be tender after all.)

Fred N. Kimmel has written eighteen Westerns. Among his works are *The Robbery at Three Wells* and *Song of the Plains* (The Macmillan Company), and *The Denver Buckaroo* (Avalon Books). He has several Westerns currently in print and another novel making the rounds in New York. Kimmel lives in Brockport, New York.

———◆———

EXCERPT FROM

Song of the Plains

As was their practice on these trips, they had camped early in the day so that the Major could have his nap before supper. By four o'clock he was slumbering gently while Joe tended the beginning of the evening meal and set a venison roast to turning on the iron spit he had unpacked.

After an hour the Major arose, stretched, and—loading a shotgun—strolled off toward a more wooded portion of the creek bottom. In another hour he was back with several small birds which he dumped down in a pile for Lupus to clean later. They would, he asserted, make a delicious breakfast in the morning. After a meal of the succulent venison the two men sat talking and sampling the fine wine the Major had brought along. The shadows were beginning to grow in length as night came steadily onward.

Published by Macmillan Publishing USA

———◆———

Venison Roast

RECIPE COURTESY OF FRED N. KIMMEL

1 (4–6 pound) venison roast	1 bay leaf
4 slices bacon	2 onions, sliced
1 tablespoon freshly ground pepper	1 cup celery, chopped
½ teaspoon thyme	3 carrots, thickly sliced
½ teaspoon savory	4 bouillon cubes
½ teaspoon marjoram	4 cups hot water
2 tablespoons salt	

Preheat oven to 325°F.

Under cold water rinse the venison and pat dry with a towel. Place venison in a deep roasting pan. Lay bacon over top. Combine pepper, thyme, savory, marjoram, and salt in a mortar and grind to release flavors and oils. Sprinkle spices over the roast.

Add bay leaf, onions, celery, carrots, bouillon cubes, and water.

Bake for 3 hours.

Serve with gravy made from the drippings and with vegetables on the side.

rthur Winfield Knight has been interested in outlaws of the nineteenth century. His stories include "Remembering the Dead," "Buffalo Horns," "Standing Alone in the Darkness," "The Secret Life of Jesse James," and a collection of poetry, *Outlaws, Lawmen and Bad Women*. Knight lives in Petaluma, California.

EXCERPT FROM

THE SECRET LIFE OF JESSE JAMES

I proposed to Zee yesterday, and she said she'd marry me.

We were sitting at the foot of the huge spruce tree we'd decorated, and the smell of the tree and the candy being made in the kitchen filled the house and I don't know that I've ever been happier.

I was rebaptized at the New Hope Baptist Church in an attempt to leave the war behind, but I can't forget it, maybe because I don't want to.

I told Zee, "At least I was alive then."

"You're alive now."

"Most of the time, I'm just pretending."

We'd gone into the kitchen and I was cranking the handle to make ice cream.

I could feel the tiredness setting in, but it wasn't the good tiredness we had after a battle with the blue bellies. It was something else. Insidious.

Zee asked, "Are you pretending now?"

It was almost dusk and my arm and chest ached and I knew I'd have to take some morphine to make it through dinner, but I kept turning the crank: bored, bored. What kind of a husband will I make? Cranking. Going through the motions.

"I've never been happier," I said.

Published by Burnhill Wolf

*Homemade
Butterscotch
Ice Cream,
page 78*

Homemade Butterscotch Ice Cream

RECIPE COURTESY OF ARTHUR WINFIELD KNIGHT

1 cup milk
1½ cups cream
½ vanilla bean or ½ teaspoon
   vanilla extract

2 whole eggs plus 2 egg yolks
½ cup sugar
¼ teaspoon salt
¼ cup butterscotch topping

In a heavy saucepan combine milk, cream, and vanilla bean. Over low heat scald the milk mix.

Remove vanilla bean and open it to release seeds; scrape seeds into milk and discard pod.

Boil water in a saucepan.

In a heat-proof mixing bowl, combine eggs and egg yolks, sugar, and salt; mix until creamy and thick. Stir in the scalded milk and cream mix.

Place bowl over the saucepan of boiling water, add scalded liquid and cook, stirring until mixture is thick enough to coat a metal spoon.

Remove saucepan and mixing bowl from heat and cool by running cold water into the saucepan, stirring ice cream mixture at the same time.

Pour ice cream into ice-cream trays (you can use metal ice cube trays with the cube dividers removed). Keep in the coldest part of your freezer until the mixture is partially frozen (35–40 minutes).

Transfer ice cream to a deep mixing bowl and whisk thoroughly with a rotary or electric mixer.

Turning the mixer to its slowest spin position, carefully add warm butterscotch topping (which has thinned as it has been kept warm in a saucepan) and blend just enough to leave a few swirls in the ice cream mix.

Transfer the ice cream back to the ice cream trays, smooth the surface of each and return them to the freezer for 2–4 hours or until frozen.

Homemade ice cream reaches its peak flavor after 4–6 hours. It's best if enjoyed within 48 hours.

Ruth Willett Lanza's work has appeared in many magazines such as *Raconteur, True West, Old West, Catholic Digest* and *Wild West.* Her short fiction was included in *New Trails,* the WWA anthology. Lanza lives in Colorado Springs, Colorado, and is always at work on a novel.

EXCERPT FROM

THE LAST ENCOUNTER

One day the two girls walked hand in hand, up the bank of the Rio Grande River. Nezbah told Felicia stories of her childhood spent on the Navajo reservation.

"Shimázan, my grandmother, lives there still in Dinetah. She lives in a hogan. And, even though she's old, she rides out every day on her pony to herd her sheep. When I visit her, she cooks mutton stew for me. And, she taught me to weave a blanket in the tradition of Dineh. She said to always leave a mistake in the weaving, where the evil spirits can escape."

"What do you mean, *Dineh* and *Dinetah?*" Felicia asked.

"*Dinetah* is the Navajo land that has been ours for centuries. *Dineh* is how we call ourselves. It means, The People."

Felicia listened with awe as Nezbah revealed her secret world. She wished she also had something interesting to tell her Navajo friend.

"Our maid, Effie, taught me to make an omelet and to bake light, fluffy biscuits. But to know how to weave a blanket is wonderful," she said.

Published by Raconteur

Shimázan's Lamb Stew

RECIPE COURTESY OF RUTH WILLETT LANZA

2 tablespoons vegetable oil
1½ pounds lamb, cubed and floured
2 cups water (if desired, red wine
    may be substituted for some
    of the water)
2 tablespoons Worcestershire sauce
2 cloves garlic, minced

dash salt
2 tablespoons finely chopped parsley
10 pearl onions
6 carrots, quartered
6 potatoes, quartered
1 cup peas (frozen will do)

Heat a deep pot and add the vegetable oil.

Brown the meat. Add the water, Worcestershire sauce, garlic, salt, and parsley.

Cover and simmer for 1 hour, or until a fork can easily penetrate the meat. Add the onions, carrots, and potatoes.

Cook slowly for 1 hour, or until vegetables are done. Add the peas and cook for 10 more minutes.

If you desire a thicker gravy, add a paste made with 1 tablespoon flour mixed with ¼ cup water.

John Legg has written over forty novels. Among his works are *Gunfight in Mescalito* and *Guns of Arizona* (Zebra Books), and *Winter Rage* (Berkley). In addition, he has one non-fiction book, *Shinin' Trails: A Possibles Bag of Fur Trade Trivia* (Eagle View Press). Legg also has contributed to the magazine trade, including *True West, Old West* and *Muzzleloader*. John Legg lives in Phoenix, Arizona.

EXCERPT FROM

GUNS OF ARIZONA

He put the rifles away and took the tin plate from Addie. He nodded his thanks and dug in, thinking how sick he was of bacon and beans.

"What're you doin'?" he asked around a mouthful of food. He had thought Addie would sit with him and eat. But she had her back to him and was working at something.

She looked over her shoulder and smiled. "Makin' us somethin' special."

"What?" Guthrie asked with growing eagerness.

"Just you never mind," she said. Her voice was more cheery than it had been in a long time.

He nodded and finished his meal. Addie finally turned and set a small Dutch oven in the fire. Then she sat next to him and ate. Guthrie sipped coffee and smoked a cigarette, feeling drowsy. He snapped out of that when Addie indicated she needed a hand getting up.

Addie waddled to the fire. Using a rag so as not to burn her hands, she pulled the Dutch oven out of the fire and set it in the dirt. She gingerly took the top off and dropped it alongside.

Guthrie perked up as the delicious aroma of apple compote wafted over him. "Well?" he said, licking his lips in anticipation.

"It's got to cool some," Addie said in a mock sternness.

He was impatient and stuck it out only a few minutes before he said, "I expect that compote's cool enough."

Addie grinned and dished some up for each of them. Guthrie attacked it, savoring its thick, gooey sweetness. It made him forget about the repetitious days of bacon and beans.

Published by Zebra Books

Apple Compote

RECIPE COURTESY OF JOHN LEGG

2 cups boiling water
1 cup sugar
½ teaspoon cinnamon
1 orange rind slice, minced
1 tablespoon dark rum
1 pound fresh apples, skinned, cored, and sliced

In a deep pan or Dutch oven, combine boiling water, sugar, cinnamon, orange rind, and rum. Return to a low boil and stir until sugar has dissolved. Reduce heat and simmer for 5 minutes.

Add apples to syrup and poach until apples are tender, but still firm. With a wooden spoon turn apples once or twice while poaching.

With 2 wooden spoons remove the apples to warmed, glass or ceramic dessert bowls.

Cover each with foil.

Return syrup to a medium boil and reduce syrup to thicken.

Pour syrup over apples and serve.

Elmore Leonard, noted today as one of the best mystery writers, got his start writing Westerns. Leonard has written over thirty novels and numerous short stories, several of which have been turned into successful films, including *3:10 to Yuma* and *Valdez Is Coming*. He has also written the screenplays for such films as *Joe Kidd* and *Mr. Majestyk*. The Western Writers of America chose his novel, *Hombre*, as one of the twenty-five best Western novels ever written. Among his other western novels are *The Bounty Hunters, Escape From Five Shadows, Last Stand at Saber River,* and *Gunsights*. Elmore Leonard lives in Birmingham, Michigan, with his wife, Joan.

EXCERPT FROM

GUNSIGHTS

"How did you keep him alive?"

The Mexican shrugged. "Tied him to a horse. He kept himself alive to Morelos. Then in the infirmary they cleaned him, sewed him together. He has a hole here," Ruben Vega said, touching his cheek, "some teeth missing"—he grinned—"part of his ear. But he's no more ugly than he was before. See, the ugliness is inside him. I say to him, 'Man, what is it like to be you? To live inside your body?' He don't know what I'm talking about. I say to him, 'Why don't you be tranquil and enjoy life more instead of rubbing against it?' He still don't know what I'm talking about, so I leave him alone . . . Well, let me think. Why didn't he die? I don't know. From Morelos I took him to my old home at Bavispe, then down to Hermosillo . . . Guaymas, we looked at the sea and ate fish . . . a long way around to come back here, but only in the beginning he was anxious to go back and saying what he's going to do to you when he finds you."

"Others tried," Bren said.

Published by Bantam Books

$$\Longrightarrow\!\!\cdot\!\!\Longleftarrow$$

Barbecued Guaymas Red Snapper
RECIPE COURTESY OF ELMORE LEONARD

1 (3-pound) red snapper
4 tablespoons lime juice
salt to taste
2 cups chopped tomatoes
1 cup chopped red onion
2 cloves garlic, minced
1 teaspoon turmeric (or achiote,
   if available)

¾ cup papaya juice
1 bay leaf
1 sprig fresh thyme (or ¼
   teaspoon dried)
2 teaspoons cilantro, minced

Clean and butterfly the snapper. Remove the bones as best you can. Sprinkle with the lime juice and a little salt. Let stand for 15 minutes.

In a blender make a paste by combining the tomatoes, onion, garlic, turmeric, papaya juice, bay leaf, thyme, and cilantro. Spread paste over both sides of the fish and refrigerate for 2 hours.

Preheat oven to 350°F.

Put the fish in a large, glass or ceramic baking dish and cover with aluminum foil. Bake for 35–45 minutes or until it flakes easily with a fork. Remove to a warmed platter.

Reserve the baking juices in a gravy boat.

Serve the fish with limes, hot chili powder, and the baking juices.

P reston Lewis, president of Western Writers of America, had an eight-year dry spell after the release of his first book, *Hard Texas Winter*. His next two novels, *New Mexico Showdown* (using the pseudonym Will Camp) and The *Lady and Doc Holliday*, finally got him back on the published trail. Among his Will Camp Westerns, published by HarperCollins, are *Tarnished Badge, Sante Fe Run, Choctaw Trail, Blood Saga, Escape from Silverton,* and others. Lewis has written three of the Bonanza series novels about the Cartwrights of the Ponderosa (Bantam). Recently he has published *The Demise of Billy the Kid, The Redemption of Jesse James,* and *Mix-up at the O.K. Corral*. Preston Lewis resides in Lubbock, Texas.

———◆———

EXCERPT FROM

THE LADY AND DOC HOLLIDAY

"Miss Deno." The voice was familiar. Spinning about, she stared into the uniform of a U.S. Cavalry captain and lifted her eyes until they met Richard's.

Lottie giggled. "I'm glad to see you, Richard, but Rachel?"

He smiled, offering his hand. "By the food."

Lottie clasped his hand and pulled him through the mingling crowd. By the bar she spotted Rachel, releasing Richard's hand when she did and hugging Rachel. "You've made me so happy by coming. I feared you might not."

Rachel nodded. "I had second thoughts about a saloon. Oh, Lottie, I've been such a fool after the hanging and all."

"It takes a while to get over those things." Lottie's voice was soothing. "No, child, let's not talk about that day."

"I can talk about the hanging now, Lottie. It no longer haunts me. Look what I brought." She stepped to the bar and lifted a towel from two pans.

Lottie laughed. "Pecan pies. And I've been wondering if you'd ever look at another pecan."

Published by Diamond Books

———◆———

Top, Gamma Lewis's Pecan Pie, page 86
Bottom, Southwest Shoofly Pie, page 125

Gamma Lewis's Pecan Pie

RECIPE COURTESY OF PRESTON LEWIS

1 cup sugar	1¾ cups pecans
¾ cup light corn syrup	⅛ teaspoon salt
½ cup margarine	1 teaspoon vanilla
3 eggs, beaten	1 (9-inch) unbaked pie crust

Preheat oven to 375°F.

In a saucepan, blend sugar, corn syrup, and margarine. Cook over medium heat, stirring constantly, until mixture comes to a boil.

In a large, glass or ceramic bowl, add the beaten eggs.

Blend hot mixture slowly with beaten eggs. Stir in pecans, salt, and vanilla. Pour into the pie shell.

Bake for 30 minutes.

Ernestine Sewell Linck is co-author with Joyce Gibson Roach of *Eats: A Folk History of Texas Foods* (Texas Christian University Press). Linck and Roach's book was the 1990 winner of the prestigious Carr P. Collins Award for Best Nonfiction from the Texas Institute of Letters. Linck's latest book, *How the Cimarron River Got Its Name and Other Stories about Coffee* was published by Republic of Texas Press.

EXCERPT FROM

EATS: A FOLK HISTORY OF TEXAS FOODS

This is the tale of the yaller bread that has traveled all over Texas:

A daughter of a settler was being married. The dinner was prepared and on the table, ready for the wedding guests. Down the trail came Old Heavypaw, a neighbor, on his way to the mill with a sack of corn. His hair looked as if the bear grease had not been washed out of it in years and his clothes looked cured, so much dirt and blood and taller from butchering had been rubbed into them. He was not one of the guests, but no one was ever sent away without being fed. He settled down to eat, helped himself to chicken, venison, greens, and potatoes, and, reaching across the table, took a big slice of pound cake. He sopped it in his gravy and devoured it in one gulp. The uneasy hostess pushed corn bread in front of him, but he shoved it aside and reached for the cake. She was really alarmed when Old Heavypaw got up, took off his belt, sat down again and resumed eating. She ran to the cooking cabin and brought back a plate of hot biscuits. "Oh, Mr. Heavypaw," she said, "do have some biscuits. We don't have them often and I know you'll like these." "No thank ye, ma'am," was his answer. "You jes' save them there biscuits for the company here. This yaller bread is good enough for me." And with that he helped himself to another big piece of the yaller bread and washed it down with a saucer of black coffee.

Published by Texas Christian University Press

Old-Fashioned Pound Cake

RECIPE COURTESY OF ERNESTINE SEWELL LINCK
AND JOYCE GIBSON ROACH

The old-fashioned way this recipe was submitted seems the best way to present it. According to the author, the cake may seem heavier when you remove it from the oven than when you put it in.

1 pound (2 cups) butter
1 pound (2 cups) sugar

1 pound (3 cups) flour
1 pound (approximately 9) eggs

Preheat oven to 300°F.

Mix butter and sugar to a cream.

Add a little flour and 1 egg at a time.

Beat well each time until all the eggs are added.

Bake in loaf or tube pan for 1 hour and 45 minutes, or until a toothpick inserted into the cake comes out dry.

Elaine Long's first novel, *Jennie's Mountain*, was released by St. Martin's Press in 1986 and was published in condensed form by Reader's Digest Book Club. The book won the WWA Medicine Pipe Bearer's Award for Best First Western Novel of 1987. Since then she has published two other books, *Bittersweet Country* and *Bear Ridge*. Long's literary honors include the National Hackeny Literary Award for Short Story and six Colorado Authors' League Top Hand Awards for novels, short stories, and specialty writing. Long lives in Buena Vista, Colorado.

EXCERPT FROM

BITTERSWEET COUNTRY

"Maggie, I'll tell you the truth. I not only don't know how much to feed a bunch of men, I don't know what to feed them. And if I have to help tie or toss fleeces, I can't see how I can be in here cooking dinner at the same time."

"A week or so before shearing, make cottage cheese every day. Hang it up in its drain cloth until it's dry. When the starving males are due, dump it in a bowl and stir in gobs of fresh cream."

"Green beans are easy. Fry several slices of bacon in a big pot, add two or three big cans of green beans and cook 'em low and slow the night before. Then just heat 'em up while you're making gravy."

Gracelyn put the pencil down with a groan. "Gravy! Maggie, do I have to have gravy?"

"Well, those men are going to want potatoes, and potatoes mean gravy."

Published by St. Martin's Press, Inc.

♦ 88 ♦ ELAINE LONG

Green Beans with Pecan Sauce and Bacon, page 90

Green Beans with Pecan Sauce and Bacon

RECIPE COURTESY OF ELAINE LONG

1 pound green beans,
  fresh or frozen
1 cup chicken broth
1 red bell pepper, diced
3 scallions, minced
1 clove garlic, minced

1 tablespoon barbecue sauce
1 drop liquid smoke flavoring
½ teaspoon salt
1 teaspoon balsamic vinegar
½ cup chopped pecans
½ cup cooked bacon, crumbled

Wash beans in cold water and, if necessary, de-string beans (if frozen, this is not required).

Cut beans into 1-inch pieces and add to a pot of boiling, salted water. There should be just enough water to cover the beans.

Simmer uncovered for 8–10 minutes, until beans are tender, but still a little crisp.

Drain in a colander and rinse with cold water.

In a skillet combine chicken broth, red bell pepper, scallions, garlic, barbecue sauce, smoke flavoring, salt, and balsamic vinegar.

Over medium heat bring mixture to a simmer, then stir for 3–4 minutes, until slightly reduced. Stir in pecans and simmer for 1 minute.

In a serving bowl, mix sauce and green beans.

Garnish with crumbled bacon.

Serve hot.

Stan Lynde is the creator of the famous syndicated comic strips *Rick O 'Shay* and *Latigo*. He also produced the self-syndicated cartoon series *Grass Roots*. His first all-text novel, *The Bodacious Kid*, has been a critical and commercial success. Lynde calls himself a "Westerner by birth and inclination" and his work aptly reflects his lifelong interest in history, lore, and legends of the American West. In addition to his receiving the Inkpot Award for achievement in the comic arts, Lynde is the recipient of the Montana Governor's Award for Arts. Lynde lives in the Flathead Valley of Montana.

EXCERPT FROM

THE BODACIOUS KID

U.S. Marshall Chance Ridgeway relaxed, but not much. He sat back in his chair and studied me with them cold blue eyes of his. "So you've been lookin' for me, have you?" he asked, and I could tell he didn't believe it for a minute. "Set down and tell me why, Merlin Fanshaw."

"Yes, sir," I said, "but I had me a *hard* night, and I haven't et in awhile. Be all right if we talk over breakfast? I'm buyin'."

"Appreciate the offer, son, but I had breakfast when it was breakfast *time*. You go ahead and eat, we'll talk after."

Well, sir, that was more than all right with me. Stripes, the waiter, handed me the bill of fare and I ordered most of what was wrote on it. "Bring me a double stack o' hotcakes," I told him, "some biscuits an' gravy, three or four eggs on the sunny side, a slab of ham, a side of sausage, a mess of fried taters, and a big pot of coffee. That orter get me started."

"Yes, I would think so," said Ridgeway, "if *I* et all that it would start *me* to a bellyache."

Published by Cottonwood Publishing

Lynda's Baking Powder Biscuits

RECIPE COURTESY OF LYNDA LYNDE

1½ cups all-purpose flour
½ cup whole wheat flour
1 tablespoon raw sugar
3½ teaspoons baking powder

1 teaspoon salt (omit if
using butter)
½ cup plus 1 tablespoon shortening
or butter
¾ cup milk

In a mixing bowl sift together flours, sugar, baking powder, and salt. Cut shortening into flour with pastry blender (or with two dinner knives) until mixture resembles pea-size texture.

With fork in hand, slowly add milk and stir together until mixture just hangs together. It will be sticky, but it is important not to overwork the dough.

Preheat oven to 450°F.

Turn biscuit dough onto lightly floured surface. Knead lightly 10–12 times. Turn over. Roll or pat to ½ inch thick. Cover with wet cloth and let dough rest for 10 minutes.

Cut dough with floured, 2½-inch, round cookie cutter (or small coffee can with both ends out).

Place biscuits on ungreased cookie sheet about 1 inch apart for crusty sides, or touching for soft sides.

Bake in center of oven for 12–15 minutes, or until golden brown.

Remove immediately from cookie sheet.

Serve with butter, jam, jelly, or honey while still warm, or store refrigerated in an air-tight container to keep fresh.

Kat Martin's historical romance novels have won numerous awards and have been published in a number of foreign languages. Among her titles are *Gypsy Lord, Sweet Vengeance, Bold Angel, Devil's Prize,* and *Midnight Rider,* all published by St. Martin's Press, Inc. Under her pseudonym, Kasey Mars, she's written *The Dream* and *The Silent Rose,* both published by Pinnacle Books. Kat Martin lives with her husband, Larry J. Martin, also a writer, near Rock Creek, outside Clinton, Montana.

EXCERPT FROM

MIDNIGHT RIDER

"Where are we going to eat?" Carly asked as he propelled her toward the door.

"My cousin Maria is in town from Santa Barbara. She wished us to join her and her daughter, Carlotta, and several other guests at the home of Ricardo Micheltorena, where she is staying during her visit." He smiled at her wickedly. "Unfortunately, I told them we would have to decline their generous invitation . . . at least for tonight. This night I would have you to myself."

A little shimmer of pleasure ran through her. "I'd really like to meet them, but I can't say I'm sorry it won't be tonight."

"You will have a chance later on."

They ate in the hotel dining room, a simple fare: an adada of chicken and red peppers, cucumbers, corn, and a guisado of beef and potatoes. Yet all of it was cooked to perfection.

Published by St. Martin's Press, Inc.

⫸⫷

Guisado Monterey (Monterey-Style Stew)
RECIPE COURTESY OF KAT MARTIN

½ cup olive oil
2 pounds sirloin tip,
   cut into ½-inch cubes
2 cups potatoes, cut into
   ½-inch cubes
2 cups coarsely chopped tomatoes
2 cloves garlic, minced
½ teaspoon cumin

¼ teaspoon oregano
1 teaspoon chile jalapeño
2 (12-ounce) bottles of beer
3 quarts beef stock
salt and pepper to taste
½ cup scallions, cut into
   1-inch pieces

Heat a heavy saucepan until a drop of water quickly sizzles away. Add olive oil and stir to coat. Add beef and potatoes; brown.

Reduce heat to a simmer; add tomatoes, garlic, cumin, and oregano. Stir for two minutes, then add chile jalapeño and beer. Cover and cook for 20 minutes.

In a separate pot, heat the beef stock. Pour beef stock into the beef and potato mixture. Season with salt and pepper.

Cover and cook for 30–40 minutes, or until beef is tender.

Add the scallions and serve.

L arry J. Martin has authored several books, including *El Lazo, Against the 7th Flag, The Devil's Bounty, The Benicia Belle, Rush to Destiny,* and *Shadow of the Grizzly,* all for Bantam Books. Martin and his wife Kat, a bestselling romance writer, live on a remote ranch road near Clinton, Montana.

≡►◈◄≡

EXCERPT FROM

BENECIA BELLE

Clint found an adobe with a small sign, Juanita's Cantina, and tied the horses to the rail in front, loosening the cinch on the gray, which had carried him the last few miles into the village. He had grazed the horses along the way, while he had been limited to the old man's small portion of frijoles and tortillas.

As soon as he pulled away the cowhide that covered the doorway, he paused, closed his eyes, and inhaled deeply in appreciation. He knew he had come to the right place. Just outside the back door of the small cafe, he saw a cooking pit with a metal grill. A variety of pots were located on the grill and the odors that emanated from there, some in roiling steam, promised what was to come.

He sat at one of the many plank tables and smiled at the approaching woman. She had obviously partaken of the succulent dishes often, since she waddled over, melon-sized breasts straining to escape from her red-dyed jerga blouse.

"Buenos dias," she said, grinning at her early customer.

"Feed me, señora, *por favor,"* Clint said simply, and the woman beamed and hurried away.

She returned with a tray of steaming delights, setting them in front of him. He recognized the tortillas and frijoles and salsa, but when he looked quizzically at the other bowls, she explained each dish with a point of a stout finger whose joints bulged.

Cordero cabazo, lamb's head; *migas,* sour bread sliced thin and fried in garlic oil until crisp; *pastel de tomal,* a pie of onion, garlic, chicken meat, beef roast, corn, tomatoes, peppers, and olives, richly spiced, and served in a masa cheese crust; *mostaza,* wild mustard greens in olive oil and garlic; *pie cerdo,* pig's feet.

Clint smiled and said, *"Con vino, por favor,"* and the woman hurried away for a mug of wine.

Published by Bantam Books

≡►◈◄≡

Pozole and Pork Chops

RECIPE COURTESY OF LARRY J. MARTIN

1½ cups water
2½ ounces cornmeal
pinch each salt and pepper
2 tablespoons olive oil
2 cups all-purpose flour
4 large pork chops
lemon pepper to taste
½ cup scallions

2 cloves garlic, minced
1 (15-ounce) can sweet corn, drained
1 (2½-ounce) can black olives, sliced
chili powder
2 medium tomatoes, chopped
2 tablespoons minced cilantro

Preheat oven to 375°F.

Make pozole (cornmeal mush) by boiling the water in a small saucepan and slowly adding cornmeal. Add salt and pepper to the mixture while stirring. (Pozole should just pour, so add water or cook down as necessary.)

Coat the pork chops with flour, then season with lemon pepper.

Add the olive oil to a large iron or oven-proof skillet.

Lightly brown the pork chops in the skillet, but don't cook them completely; that comes later. Set the pork chops aside on paper towels to drain.

There should be oil left in the skillet; if not, add some, then sauté the scallions and garlic, all the while de-glazing the skillet.

Remove the skillet from the heat and add the pozole, corn, and olives; blend all together.

Smooth out the pozole mixture and cover with a light coating of chili powder. Top with a layer of tomatoes, then with another coating of chili powder.

Add the pork chops. Sprinkle them with cilantro and bake for 30–40 minutes, or until they are nicely browned and supple.

oe Megeath's publications include numerous professional pieces related to business, geology, and mining and minerals. His Western article "They Shouldn't Have Taken His Rope" appeared in *True West* magazine, and his article "The Wooly West" appeared in *Wild West* magazine. Megeath also writes for various newspapers including *The Rocky Mountain News*. Megeath lives in Encampment, Wyoming.

EXCERPT FROM

THE WOOLY WEST

The battle of sheep for their place on the Western range was a bloody and prolonged affair. Long after the Indian Wars had ended, even after World War I, the bloody contest between sheepmen and cattlemen continued. From the 1870's to the 1920's raids of various types and magnitude were waged against sheep in the western states.

. . . (Many) factors were important in creating the sheep-cattle wars. One comes to realize, though, that it was a cultural war . . . almost a religious war. Strong people attracted to the extroverted environment of cattle maintained a macho or physical prowess that fit with the world of the wild longhorns. Even when tempered by Hereford and Shorthorn breeds on the open ranges, the image still existed. It is hard to imagine a Christmas carol that begins, "While cowboys watched their herds at night."

Strong people attracted to the more docile and vulnerable environment of the sheep maintained a patient, caring nature that fit with the caretaking required by their charges. It is hard to imagine a gripping story revolving around a sheep stampede.

Cattle and sheep can range perfectly together. The people that owned them and handled them often had trouble.

By refusing to eat sheep the cattlemen not only missed out on some good grub, but also a way to get rid of the varmints.

Published by Wild West Magazine

Savory Leg of Lamb

RECIPE COURTESY OF JOE MEGEATH

1 (6–7 pound) leg of lamb
2 cloves garlic, minced
2 tablespoons lime juice

1 dash Tabasco sauce
¼ teaspoon salt
10–12 pimento-stuffed olives

Wash and pat dry the leg of lamb.

In a small bowl combine garlic, lime juice, Tabasco, and salt.

With a paring knife, cut a wide, deep "X" into the meat. Using the tip of the paring knife, hold open a hole along a slice of the "X" and add some of the lime mixture. Plug the hole with an olive to seal it. Two or three inches away, open another hole along the "X" and repeat the process until you have used all the olives and the lime mixture. Rub any leftover mixture onto the meat.

Place the leg of lamb in the refrigerator for at least 4 hours or overnight. Preheat oven to 350°F.

Roast the leg of lamb for 3 hours, or 30 minutes per pound.

After removing the roast, let it set for 10–15 minutes for easy carving. Slice it on a bias.

Drippings make an excellent gravy.

andy Moulton is the author of many award-winning Wyoming-based historical works. Her first book, *Steamboat: Legendary Bucking Horse*, co-authored with her mother-in-law, Flossie Moulton, was published in 1992 by High Plains Press. She has also published two works for a new history/travel series, *Roadside History of Wyoming* and *Roadside History of Nebraska* (both from Mountain Press Publishing Company). Her new book, *Wagon Wheels*, earned her the Friend of the Trail Award from the Old West Trail Foundation, and a Heritage Award from the Wyoming Historical Society. Moulton is a staff writer for *Persimmon Hill,* the National Cowboy Hall of Fame's publication, and a regular contributor to *American Cowboy Magazine.* Moulton, when not on the historical trail, lives in Encampment, Wyoming.

⇒◆⇐

EXCERPT FROM

ROADSIDE HISTORY OF WYOMING

Winter didn't start particularly early; the first major storm of the season blew in from the west on January 9, 1887. Another hit January 11. Three days later stockmen rode through sixteen inches of snow, forging through and around drifts twelve to fifteen feet high, wondering how their cattle were faring.

At the end of January the temperature rose and the snow began to soften, but it stayed warm only long enough for some of the snow to melt and form pools of water. Then the temperature plummeted again, freezing the water and covering the land with a sheet of ice that made it nearly impossible for cattle to eat. February was just as cold and snowy as January, and not until late March did the storms abate. Cowboys called that miserable winter the Great Die-Up. Thousands of head of cattle perished—stacked frozen against the fences put in place by the homesteaders—and so did a way of life.

Published by Mountain Press Publishing Company

⇒◆⇐

Candy's Spudnuts

RECIPE COURTESY OF CANDY MOULTON

Spudnuts are a form of doughnut. A certain amount of baked potato is added to change the flavor of the dough slightly and give the fare its unique name.

2 cups milk
1½ packages fast-rising
  dry yeast
½ cup warm water
1 teaspoon salt
½ cup sugar
⅔ cup shortening

2 teaspoons vanilla extract
1 cup mashed potatoes
  (do not use instant potatoes)
2 eggs, beaten
6 cups flour
lard or vegetable oil for frying

Scald milk and cool to warm.

In a large bowl dissolve the yeast in lukewarm water.

Combine salt, sugar, and shortening with the milk, then add to yeast mix.

Add vanilla, potatoes, eggs, 3 cups of the flour to the mix. Add the remaining flour and knead until you have a soft dough. (Add more flour if needed.)

Roll out dough to a half inch thick, and cut spudnuts into doughnut shape, using a doughnut cutter. Save the holes. Let spudnuts and holes rise in a warm place for about an hour.

Heat lard to 350°F. Fry the spudnuts and holes in the hot lard, turning once, until golden brown on both sides. Be sure to push the spudnuts and holes down into the lard so both the tops and bottoms will cook.

Drain on a paper towel.

Spudnuts are best glazed. To make glaze, mix one tablespoon of powdered sugar with 1 teaspoon of vanilla and enough boiling water, about a cup or so, to make a thin frosting. Dip each spudnut in the glaze then eat them hot: That's when they are the best.

You can roll the hot spudnuts and holes in sugar or put sugar in a paper bag, add a few spudnuts and holes, and shake to coat them.

Joan Lowery Nixon is the author of over one hundred books, many of them garnering awards: the Steck-Vaughn Award, from the Texas Institute of Letters, for *The Alligator Under the Bed*; and Edgar Allen Poe awards for *The Kidnapping of Christina Lattimore*, *The Seance*, and *The Other Side of Dark*. Her ventures into historical fiction, *A Family Apart* and *In The Face of Danger*, brought her two WWA Spur Awards. Nixon lives in Houston, Texas.

EXCERPT FROM

IN THE FACE OF DANGER

[Megan] added another log to the fire. . . . Then she swung the arm holding the apple mixture back over the fire and began to stir it slowly with the wooden paddle, just as she'd seen Emma do.

When the apples were finally cooked to a deep brown thickness, Megan brought Emma a sample. With the tip of one finger, Emma warily skimmed the glob Megan held out on the paddle. She tasted it and smiled. "That's it," she said. "Take it off the fire, and stir it now and then as long as the pan is hot, just to keep it from sticking."

Megan scooped a finger along the top of the apple butter, too, waved it quickly, and popped it into her mouth. "It's good!" she said with such surprise that Emma laughed.

"Of course it's good. Couldn't you tell by the way it smells?"

Megan shrugged and stirred the paddle once around the pot. "It's brown and strange-looking. I didn't know what to expect."

"You'll like it on your bread," Emma said. "We'll have it all winter."

Published by Bantam Doubleday Dell

—————≫◆≪—————

◆ 100 ◆ JOAN LOWERY NIXON

Apple Butter,
page 102

Apple Butter

RECIPE COURTESY OF JOAN LOWERY NIXON

4 pounds Jonathan apples, washed, skinned, cored, and quartered	juice and grated rind of one lemon
2 cups apple cider (or water)	1 teaspoon cinnamon
1 cup sugar	½ teaspoon ground cloves
	½ teaspoon allspice

In a large pot or Dutch oven, combine apples and cider and cook slowly until apples are soft.

Strain the mixture, then add remaining ingredients.

Cook at medium to low heat, stirring often, until mixture thickens enough to fall in sheets from the spoon.

Cool, then pour into scalded jelly glasses and seal with paraffin.

Serve as a spread on bread.

Jim Palmer is the author of *Game Wardens vs. Poachers: Tickets Still Available* (Krause Publications). A retired game warden, he lives and writes at his home in the mountains above Silver City, New Mexico.

EXCERPT FROM

GAME WARDENS VS. POACHERS: TICKETS STILL AVAILABLE

Grinning, Wally opened a cooler in the trunk of the car and removed a big globular wad wrapped in plastic. "Chili," he says, "all we gotta do is melt it and we eat."

But his smile vanished and he began cussing when he discovered he'd forgotten to pack a pot to cook in. In only a few seconds he came up with a solution; he pried a hub cap off a rear wheel of the car. Then he pulled out the tail of the shirt he'd been wearing for a week and used it to wipe some of the dust and grit out of the vessel. With a triumphant giggle, he tossed his makeshift pot in the fire and dumped in the contents of the plastic bag.

Sure enough, it melted and turned into chili, which we scooped out of the hub cap with tin coffee cups. Like everything else old Wally prepared, it was wonderful. But we were thankful for the starless night, so we didn't have to look at the stuff which was surely floating in it.

Published by Krause Publications

Nine-Raisin Rice

RECIPE COURTESY OF JIM PALMER, A FRIEND OF OLD WALLY

Until the day he died, Old Wally kept secret his recipe for what became known around the warden force as "Hubcap Chili." But one day, in a moment of weakness, he did share with me the makins' of another of his exotic dishes, and I'm going to let you in on it.

¾ cup wild rice (use only genuine wild rice and not the mixed type)	*9 raisins*
	3 mushrooms, sliced
4 strips bacon, diced	*1 (15-ounce) can mushroom soup*
1 small onion, diced	*½ teaspoon each salt and pepper*

Boil the rice in a large saucepan for 1 hour (add 20 minutes for higher altitudes); drain the rice.

Sauté the bacon, onion, and raisins until the onions are translucent and limp.

Preheat oven to 350°F.

In an 8-inch-square casserole dish, combine the rice, sautéed mixture, and sliced mushrooms; mix thoroughly.

Pour the mushroom soup over the top. Add salt and pepper.

Cover and bake for 1 hour.

Choral Pepper, a good friend of the infamous Erle Stanley Gardner and the former owner and editor of *Desert Magazine,* has written for the *Los Angeles Times, Christian Science Monitor,* and various other publications. Pepper has written over fifteen books, including *Treasure Legends of the West* (Gibbs Smith). Choral Pepper lives in Coronado, California.

━━◆◆◆◆━━

EXCERPT FROM

TREASURE LEGENDS OF THE WEST

Nummel purposefully crossed Yuma Wash in the Trigos while the sun was still low and continued on in a southeasterly direction. When he met the old Indian trail, he followed it for awhile, and then broke off into untried terrain to pursue his own contemplated shortcut. At high noon, he sank gratefully against the bank of an arroyo shaded by a big paloverde tree. There he ate a sandwich and drank the remaining water in his canteen. This would have been foolhardy with fifty-odd miles yet to walk, but Nummel calculated that the natural water tank couldn't be more than a mile distant. There had been a recent summer storm. It would be full of fresh water.

Nummel had been a prospector most of his life. Whenever he noticed an outcrop of quartz, no matter how unpromising, he chipped off a sample with his prospector's pick. He now mechanically hacked off a chunk of dirty yellow quartz from a ledge on the bank of the wash beside him.

Published by Gibbs Smith Publisher

━━◆◆◆◆━━

Pepper's Dutch-Oven Cornbread Casserole

RECIPE COURTESY OF CHORAL PEPPER

This recipe can be made at home in the oven or at a campsite in a Dutch oven. In either case, the cornmeal mush, requiring lots of water, should be prepared in your kitchen. You'll probably have extra cornmeal squares leftover. They can be fried on a griddle or in a skillet and served with eggs or however you wish.

2 cups yellow cornmeal
3 cups water
3 tablespoons dehydrated onion
2 tablespoons vegetable oil
½ teaspoon paprika

1 (12-ounce) can chile con carne without beans (2 cans if you're using a large Dutch oven)
1 (12-ounce) can corn, whole kernel, drained (2 cans if you're using a large Dutch oven)

In a deep saucepan combine cornmeal, water, dehydrated onion, vegetable oil, and paprika. Bring to a boil, then reduce to a simmer and, stirring constantly, cook for about 6 minutes or until the mixture is a very thick mush. (It's important to have the cornmeal absorb as much of the moisture as possible.)

Pour into a broiler pan or large shallow casserole dish.

Refrigerate until firm. Cut into 3-inch squares. Individually wrap squares in plastic wrap and, if you're going to use them at a campsite, repackage them in sealable plastic bags or containers. For home use, wrap in plastic and freeze, or refrigerate and use within two days.

At the campsite:

Place a layer of cornmeal squares in an oiled Dutch oven.

Cover the squares with a can of chile con carne and a can of whole kernel corn.

Top with another layer of squares. If you have a large Dutch oven, add another layer of squares, chile, and corn, then top with a layer of squares.

With lid in place, put the Dutch oven on a bed of campfire coals and cover the lid with more coals. Bake for 45 minutes.

At home:

Preheat oven to 350°F.

Prepare squares, chile con carne, and corn as detailed above.

Bake, covered, for 30 minutes.

Remove cover and bake for 15 more minutes to form a nice, crunchy crust.

Gwen Petersen is a very funny lady. She has written several books, including *The Ranch Woman's Manual, The Bachelor from Hell, Howling with the Wolves, Scratch Where It Itches, Not Where It Looks Best* and *Cow Camp Cookery*. And, as a writer of cowboy poetry, she was chosen to represent Montana at the Cowboy Poetry Gathering in Elko, Nevada. Petersen currently writes a syndicated newspaper column called "In a Sow's Ear." She lives in Big Timber, Montana.

EXCERPT FROM

Cow Camp Cookery

A cowboy can put away grub
As though he were built like a tub,
But he's thin as a rail
As he rides down the trail,
And the cook is the one they call, "Chub."

Oh, a diet of biscuits and beans
Can become an explosive of means,
And that may be why
When old cowboys die
They only find tatters of jeans.

Cowboys like coffee that's black
And sturdy enough to attack
They brew it and brew it
Until they can chew it—
It tastes just like tar and shellac.

The people who dearly love chicken soup
Have probably not cleaned a chicken coop.
Do you think they would savor it
If they knew that their favorite
Was started among all that chicken poop?

The ranchwoman got out her jars,
And peeled and pickled for hours,
Which made her so tired
She thought she'd expired,
But revived after nine whiskey sours.

Published by Sow's Ear Press

Sourdough Starter & Sourdough Pancakes

RECIPE COURTESY OF GWEN PETERSEN

Plan to start this recipe a week in advance. The sourdough starter in this recipe can be used for bread, muffins, and biscuits, as well.

Starter:

> ½ package active dry yeast
> 2½ cups lukewarm water
> 1 tablespoon sugar
> 2 cups flour

Pancakes:

> 1 cup sourdough starter
> 2 cups lukewarm water
> 2½ cups flour
> 3 tablespoon sugar
> 1 egg

> 2 tablespoons cooking oil
> ¼ cup evaporated milk
> 1 teaspoon salt
> 1 teaspoon baking soda

Starter:

Dissolve the yeast in ½ cup of the lukewarm water. Add remaining water, sugar, and flour. Mix well.

Let the mixture stand in a covered bowl or crock (not metal) for three days at room temperature. Stir down daily.

Refrigerate after three days. The starter, or sponge as it's called by some, is now ready to use.

Pancakes:

The night before you make the pancakes, put 1 cup of starter in a large, glass, plastic or ceramic bowl (return the remaining starter to the refrigerator). To the cup of starter add lukewarm water, flour, and 1 table-spoon of the sugar. Mix well. The mixture will be thick and lumpy. Cover the bowl and set it in a warm place (not hot!) overnight.

In the morning, take 1 or 2 cups of batter from the bowl and put it in the starter jar that's been stored in the refrigerator. (Each time you set out sourdough starter overnight, always put a cup or two back in the refrigerated starter jar. This keeps the sourdough starter fresh and available for its next use.)

Add to the batter remaining in the bowl the egg, cooking oil, and evaporated milk. Mix thoroughly.

In a small mixing bowl sift together salt, baking soda, and remaining sugar.

Fold gently into batter. This causes a foaming and rising action. Allow to stand for a few minutes, then spoon pancakes onto a hot, greased griddle. Sourdough requires a hotter griddle than conventional pancakes.

If batter seems too thick, add a small amount of cream or milk.
*Never add more flour to your fermented base except as detailed in the recipe.
Starter can remain in refrigerator for years as long as it's used occasionally
and refreshed as above.*

G eorge Post writes scientific journals and textbooks, as well as features for *The Monthly Arizonian* (Tubac, Arizona), *Nogales International* (Nogales, Arizona) and other Southwestern newspapers. In addition, he's done several articles for magazines such as *Lapidary Journal*. His nonfiction book *Out of the Fast Lane* was published by Dorrance Publishing. Post is presently working on several novels and nonfiction young-adult books. Post lives in Rio Rico, Arizona.

EXCERPT FROM

OUT OF THE FAST LANE

This excerpt describes cooking for as many as fifty people working to stop an anthrax outbreak in moose and cattle in western Wyoming. All the cattle ranchers from the area pitched in to give antibiotics to living cattle and to pile wood on, and burn, dead cattle and moose.

Ell, Rachel Taylor, Sara Birch and two other women came a little later in the day. Ell brought large cooking pots and other equipment left over from her Syndicate days. She and all the ladies cooked huge pots of stew, beans, other boiled vegetables and barbecue beef, all served with tossed salads, bread and other items. Most of the ladies were amazed at how Ell could put such a thing together in such a short time, until she explained how many times she had done the same things over and over for nearly 15 years when she and Bert worked in Texas. All the men and boys working on wood details, or with crews dosing cattle, agreed they had "never had better vittles," which made Ell proud.

Published by Dorrance Publishing Co., Inc.

One-Pot Chop Suey

RECIPE COURTESY OF GEORGE POST

Serve over rice or chow mein noodles.

1 tablespoon vegetable oil
2 pounds pork shoulder or beef chuck (cut in 1–1½ inch chunks)
1 tablespoon soy sauce
1 cube beef bouillon (or 1 teaspoon liquid bouillon)
1 cup water
2 cups (4 large stalks) chopped celery
½ cup (1 medium) chopped onion
½ cup (1 medium) chopped green or red bell peppers
1 pound soybean sprouts
1 teaspoon salt
2 tablespoons corn starch dissolved in ¼ cup cold water
½ cup boiled Chinese-style rice

Heat a large pot or Dutch oven and add the vegetable oil. Cook the meat, turning occasionally, until brown on all sides. Spoon off excess fat.

Add soy sauce and stir, then add the beef bouillon and water. Stir to dissolve the bouillon.

Add celery, onion, bell pepper, and soybean sprouts. Cook until vegetables are just slightly crisp. Add salt and corn starch. Stir until well mixed and starting to thicken.

Ellen Recknor has published several books, including the popular and award-winning *Me and the Boys* and *Leaving Missouri*. Recknor also has several romance titles under her pseudonym Ellen Archer, including *Taboo*, *Darling*, and *Tiger Lil'*. Recknor lives in Scottsdale, Arizona

EXCERPT FROM

ME AND THE BOYS

"I read about you," I said. "In *Ghost Ruggles: Phantom of the White Sands Wasteland!* Did you really hold off all those Kiowa single-handed?"

He looked at me like I'd gone crazy. "What Kiowa?"

"The ones that attacked you along the Rio Vermejo! There were twenty bloodthirsty braves against you, and you licked 'em all!"

He pointed at my dessert, of which I'd only eaten half. "Shame to waste that pecan pie," he said. I pushed it toward him.

"Seems I got a terrible sweet tooth in my old age," he mumbled, his mouth full. "Must be a tapeworm. That book didn't tell you no truth, missy. I never been up the Rio Vermejo. Only dealin's I've had with the Kiowa have been peaceable. Near cordial, accordin' to Kiowa standards." The last gooey pecan went into his mouth. "That whole book full'a such nonsense?"

Published by Berkeley Publishing Group

My Pecan Pie
RECIPE COURTESY OF ELLEN RECKNOR

1¼ cups all-purpose flour, plus
  some for handling dough
4 tablespoons shortening, chilled
2 tablespoons butter, chilled and
  diced into small cubes
pinch salt
4 tablespoons ice water
4 eggs

2 cups dark corn syrup
½ cup maple syrup
  (imitation will do)
2 tablespoons butter, melted
2 teaspoons vanilla
1 tablespoon finely minced
  orange rind
2 cups pecan halves

In a large mixing bowl, combine the flour, shortening, butter, and salt. Blend together with a pastry knife until slightly grainy, then, with your fingertips, rub the mixture together until it forms flakes like coarse meal. Add the ice water and, again with your fingertips, blend until the water is absorbed.

When the flour mixture can be formed into a dough ball, dust lightly with more flour, wrap in plastic wrap or wax paper and chill for 30–45 minutes.

Preheat the oven to 400°F.

On a large floured surface, roll out the dough into a 12-inch to 14-inch circle and about ⅛-inch thick.

Lightly butter a 9-inch pie plate. Using the rolling pin, lift the pie dough and unroll it over the pie plate—there should be an extra inch or two hanging over the sides and the dough should have plenty of slack in the middle. With your fingers gently tuck the dough to form with the inside of the pie plate. Trim the remaining dough from the edge of the pie plate, leaving an extra half-inch. Fold the extra under to make a double thickness around the plate. Cover the dough with a sheet of foil that has been buttered on the side facing the pie dough and formed in the shape of the pie plate. Do not prick the dough, or the filling will run out when it is added later. Bake the pie shell for 8 minutes, then remove the shell to cool and discard the foil.

In a large bowl, beat the eggs with an electric beater. Slowly add the corn syrup and then the maple syrup until well blended; then blend in the melted butter, vanilla, and orange rind. Finally, with a spatula, stir in the pecans.

Add the filling to the pie shell and bake in the middle of the oven for 35–40 minutes or until the filling is firm.

Serve warm or cooled to room temperature.

Joyce Gibson Roach is a three-time WWA Spur Award winner in both fiction and nonfiction. Her published titles include "A Two Gun Man" in *New Trails*, "The Cowgirls," and "A High-toned Woman" in *Hoein' the Short Rows*, and "Just as I Am" from the *Women of the West*. She and co-author Ernestine Sewell Linck shared the Texas Institute of Letters nonfiction book prize for *Eats: A Folk History of Texas Foods* (Texas Christian University Press). Her latest book is *Wind Rose: A Folk History of a Cross Timbers Settlement*. Roach lives in Keller, Texas.

⤝⬥⤞

EXCERPT FROM

A TWO GUN MAN

Lee Barclay, alias Fudge, of mysterious origins and mixed parentage, comes to Crosswinds Ranch with his father when he is little more than a baby. Left with the owner's wife, Ruth, much of the time, Fudge learns about cows, horses, guns and "table."

Sometimes the cowboys would take their ease about the bunkhouse late in the evenings when they returned from chores done for Mr. Richards, things such as building fence or moving cattle from one place to another, or doctoring stock. After supper around the big table in Mrs. Richards's backyard, the men would take their plates and utensils to a big washtub of soapy water, wash them out in one bucket, rinse them in another and stack them in yet another. They were free to lollygag—that's what Mrs. Richards called it—but she laughed and Fudge knew that what they did was approved. Fudge did the same, sharing the good food, observing the table manners of the men practiced under Mrs. Richards's watchful eye, only he had to empty the water buckets and tidy up, as Mrs. Richards called it, after the men finished. It was the one time of the day they were under the stern hand of a high-toned woman, but to be able to get such eats on a ranch, to have canned peaches at every meal and a feast on Sunday was worth enduring prayer, napkins, two utensils, table etiquette and dish washing. That's what the boys all said, although Fudge had never known life to be any other way.

Published by Bantam Books

⤝⬥⤞

Ranch-Style Peach Cobbler

RECIPE COURTESY OF JOYCE GIBSON ROACH

This outstanding recipe can be cooked in the oven or in a Dutch oven over a campfire.

1 cup sugar	1 stick (¼ pound) butter
1 cup flour	2 (20-ounce) cans peaches
1 teaspoon baking powder	and syrup
pinch salt	cream to garnish

Outdoor method:
   In a mixing bowl, combine sugar, flour, baking powder, and salt to make a batter.
   Melt the butter in a Dutch oven. Add the batter, then add the peaches and syrup.
   Place the Dutch oven on a bed of coals. Put the lid on the Dutch oven and add coals to the lid. Cook for about 45 minutes, or until the top gets a deep, golden brown.

Oven method:
   Preheat oven to 375°F.
   Make batter as described above.
   Coat the sides and bottom of a baking dish with melted butter.
   Add the batter, then add the peaches and syrup.
   Bake, uncovered, for 45 minutes, or until top is a deep, golden brown.

   Please use nothing but cream for garnish. No substitute will taste as good. And, serve in bowls, not on plates—this is ranch food.

Mark Roberts has published over 180 novels, the majority being traditional, historical, and adult Westerns, with twenty-nine men's adventures, thirteen military adventures, one science fiction, and one biography. His publishers include Avon, Ballantine, Pinnacle, Warner, Chelsea House, and Zebra. Roberts lives in Tampa, Kansas.

EXCERPT FROM

GALLOWS RIDERS

Riney and Perk turned abruptly, hands going to their sixguns at the sound of footsteps pounding on the boardwalk outside. They relaxed when Marv Hoyle entered.

"Hey, Perk, you were sure right about that *mañana* business!" The collective frowns of the gang quieted the rest of Marv's report. "Those Mezkin soldiers made camp for the night not ten miles outside town. We can easily overtake them and be to the canyon first." Marv looked away from Riney to each of the others, seeking support. "We'll even have time to get ol' Charlie free."

Marv joined the gang and accepted a glass of tequila from Davey. The bartender appeared in the doorway, bearing a large platter filled with slices of apple, jicama, and bananas, seasoned lightly with mild chile powder, lime juice, and grated coconut. "Here, Señores, a few bocadillos to increase the enjoyment of your drinking. Compliments of the Cantina Rosales."

"Mighty nice of you," Davey replied after translating the barkeep's words for the gang. He started to turn, then froze, his hand darting toward his holster.

"No, Señor! That would be a . . . how you say?. . . fatal mistake." The rattling of beads announced Padilla's entrance to the barroom. He held a double barrel shotgun at his waist level, centered on Davey's middle. He kept his eyes on Davey while he addressed the others.

"That's right, *hombres,* I do not wish trouble, however I came prepared."

Published by Zebra Books

Bocadillos Mejicanos
(Mexican Appetizers),
page 116

Bocadillos Mejicanos (Mexican Appetizers)

RECIPE COURTESY OF MARK ROBERTS

lettuce leaves
1 large red apple (Jonathan or Rome), cored and thinly sliced
1 large green apple (Granny Smith), cored and thinly sliced
1 medium jicama, peeled and thinly sliced
1 medium papaya, seeded and sliced into thin strips
4 medium bananas, peeled, split length-wise, and cut in 1-inch sections
1 medium cantaloupe, peeled, seeded, and thinly sliced
⅓ cup fresh lime juice
¼ cup grated coconut
2 tablespoons chile pasilla (dark chili powder)
½ teaspoon cayenne (optional)

While preparing ingredients, chill a large platter.

On the chilled platter arrange a bed of lettuce leaves. Arrange the apple slices in a ring around outside edge of leaves, alternating red and green slices, with some white meat showing (colors of the Mexican flag). For the second ring (on the lettuce), alternate jicama, papaya, banana, and cantaloupe; then make another ring of apple. Fill to center with remaining fruit.

Drizzle lime juice on all the fruit. Sprinkle with coconut, chile pasilla, and cayenne.

JoAnn Roe is noted for her popular children's books featuring Marco the Manx. Among these titles are *Castaway Cat, Fisherman Cat, Alaska Cat,* and *Samurai Cat,* all published by Montevista Press. In addition, Roe has published several nonfiction books, including *The Columbia River, Seattle Uncovered, Stevens Pass Ghost Towns & Boom Towns* (also by Montevista Press) and *The North Cascadians,* published by Madrona Publishers. Roe lives in Bellingham, Washington.

EXCERPT FROM

THE NORTH CASCADIANS

In 1921, a notorious whiskey runner, Red Prince, was shot dead at the border after shooting a customs man. Two years later, Okanogan County Sheriff E. J. Wilson and his deputy, B. McCauley, set a trap for a known ring operating near Riverside. Seven cars moving confidently along a road were intercepted whereupon the passengers opened fire on the sheriff with repeating rifles. The sheriff and his deputy captured five of the men, shot one unintentionally, and chased the rest as far as the next county. In the captured cars there was not only bottled liquor but stills, coils, moonshine, and 200 gallons of mash. One of the captured men was highly indignant, declaring that he had paid "someone" in county government $500 for clear passage.

Published by Madrona Publishers

Prohibition Bean Dip

RECIPE COURTESY OF JOANN ROE

1 (16-ounce) can refried beans
1 cup sour cream
1 cup salsa, medium heat
1 (4-ounce) can black olives, pitted and sliced
½ cup (1 medium) red bell pepper, chopped
tortilla chips for dipping

In a blender combine all ingredients and blend until the olives and peppers are still somewhat chunky.

Serve with tortilla chips.

Patti Sherlock is best noted for her popular *Four of a Kind* (Holiday House), a Spur runner-up. In addition, she has published two other books, *Alone on the Mountain* (Doubleday) and *Some Fine Dogs* (Holiday House). Sherlock free-lances to several magazines including *High Country News* and *Farm and Ranch Magazine*. She lives on a farm outside Idaho Falls, Idaho.

⇒•◦•⇐

EXCERPT FROM

FOUR OF A KIND

"Grandpa, the place is full. The food must be good."

"Pa said them Chinese 'at worked the mines up at Caribou City used 'ta eat dogs."

"That was a long time ago! There're laws against that now." I was wishing Grandpa wouldn't talk so loud.

A petite Chinese waitress came up and asked our order. Grandpa stared at her so long I grew embarrassed and hastily ordered the Sunday special for both of us.

After she left Grandpa hissed. "Did ya see the hands on that girl? They was smaller'n a kindygartner's. Good thing she works in a Chinese restaurant. Them hands wouldn't hardly fit around a big bakin' potata." I moved my chair and peered out the window, hoping it would seem like I wasn't with Grandpa. I was sure everyone in both dining rooms could hear him.

When the girl delivered our food, Grandpa peered over the table at her feet.

"Yep!" he cried as she moved toward the kitchen. "Feet're the same way. Little as sheep hooves. Ya couldn't depend on 'em ta take ya no distance atall. I like a substantial foot. Used to have a geldin' with feet like dishpans. I could git on that horse n' travel . . ."

I was so anxious to get out of there I wolfed down my food without tasting it.

Published by Holiday House

⇒•◦•⇐

Black Walnut and Ginger Shrimp Stir Fry

RECIPE COURTESY OF PATTI SHERLOCK

The best way to prepare this dish is in a wok, although a deep, heavy skillet will do.

1 pound medium shrimp, peeled and de-veined
1 tablespoon rice vinegar
4 tablespoons soy sauce
¼ teaspoon garlic powder
¼ cup orange juice
2½ teaspoons cornstarch
1 teaspoon sugar

dash chile oil or hot sauce
2 tablespoons sesame or vegetable oil
1 teaspoon grated ginger root
4 green onions cut in 1-inch lengths
½ cup black walnuts, coarsely chopped
4 cups rice, cooked fluffy

In a colander wash the shrimp, then cover with a damp cloth to keep moist.

In a bowl stir together rice vinegar, soy sauce, garlic powder, orange juice, cornstarch, sugar, and chile oil or hot sauce. Set aside.

Heat a wok until a drop of water quickly sizzles away (medium-high heat). Add the sesame or vegetable oil and swirl to coat.

Add ginger root, green onions, and walnuts. Stir-fry for about one minute, then add shrimp and stir-fry until the shrimp are just starting to turn pink.

Quickly make a well in the middle of the wok. Give the prepared sauce a stir, then add it to the wok.

Cook and stir until sauce starts to thicken. Serve over rice.

Author W. M. Shockley has published many articles in magazines and journals. Some of his recent work, such as "Bust Out," "The Left Flank," and "Water," appeared in *Louis L'Amour Magazine*. Shockley lives in Riverside, California.

⟫⟪

EXCERPT FROM

BUST OUT

He hadn't let Reuben see the Winchester before today, but he was hungry for some meat. He held the rifle to his shoulder and waited for a squirrel. It didn't take long—the squirrels were everywhere on the trees. He'd seen a few deer skittish in the woods but none close enough to shoot. He didn't feel like dressing a deer anyway. Not with the coast so close.

He aimed and fired, blew the head clean off.

"Meat does fall off trees!" Reuben said with a laugh as the headless squirrel landed a few feet from him. "Not much to eat on this thing." Merle expected that Reuben would have been more upset by the dead squirrel, but he wasn't.

The squirrel wasn't much, but it was a damn sight better than what they had been eating. Served with rice and beans it made a pretty good meal.

Published by Louis L'Amour Western Magazine

⟫⟪

Pan-Fried Squirrel
RECIPE COURTESY OF W. M. SHOCKLEY

½ cup salt in 2 quarts water	*¼ teaspoon dry mustard*
4 squirrels, cleaned and quartered	*¼ teaspoon celery seed*
3 eggs, beaten	*¼ teaspoon onion powder*
¼ cup evaporated milk	*¼ teaspoon salt*
½ cup flour	*¼ teaspoon pepper*
½ cup cornmeal	*1 cup lard or shortening*
¼ teaspoon oregano	

Soak the squirrel for 4 hours or overnight in the brine.

In a bowl combine the eggs and evaporated milk.

In a deep paper sack combine flour, cornmeal, and spices.

Dredge the squirrel quarters in the egg mixture; then, two quarters at a time, add to the flour bag and shake vigorously to coat. Continue until all quarters are coated.

Heat a Dutch oven or large, deep skillet until a drop of water quickly sizzles away. Add the lard or shortening and fry the squirrel quarters.

Drain on a cloth or paper towels.

Serve with buiscuits. Drippings make an excellent gravy.

R ichard Slatta is the author of *The Cowboy Encyclopedia* (ABC-CLIO), one of several major reference books for Old West aficionados. *The Cowboy Encyclopedia* is a powerful reference piece full of lively jargon, situations, and wherewithal that made up the life of the infamous Western cowboy. Slatta lives in Cary, North Carolina.

EXCERPT FROM

THE COWBOY ENCYCLOPEDIA

While riding the range, a cowboy's noon dinner might include some dried beef, dried fruit, sourdough biscuits, and perhaps a cup of coffee if he carried a pot in his saddlebags. According to cowhand Philip Ashton Rollins (*The Cowboy*, 1922), the bare necessities rolled into a slicker might include a "frying-pan, some flour, bacon, coffee, salt, and, as a substitute for yeast, either a bottle of sour dough or a can of baking-powder."

Meals at camp or at the bunkhouse offered greater variety and abundance. Pauline Barham cooked for Chapman-Barnard hands in Oklahoma during the 1940s. She recalled the following:

"They were hungry. They would eat everthing, and they enjoyed it. Beef roast and beans is the main thing for cowboys, I think. Hot biscuits. We made our own biscuits. And potatoes fixed some way. Always coffee. The coffee pot was on all the time."

Published by ABC-CLIO

Bunkhouse Beans

RECIPE COURTESY OF RICHARD SLATTA

1 cup pinto beans, sorted
    and cleaned
1 cup black beans, sorted
    and cleaned
4 cups water
3 cups chicken broth
1 cup coarsely chopped onion
3 cloves garlic, minced
½ pound pork chops, deboned
    and coarsely chopped (or bacon
    slab with rind, chopped)

2 tablespoons tomato puree
½ cup (1 medium) coarsely
    chopped green bell pepper
1 tablespoon chili powder
½ tablespoon cumin
½ teaspoon oregano
large pinch cayenne or red pepper
½ teaspoon dry mustard
1 bay leaf
3 tablespoons dark molasses
¼ teaspoon salt

In a Dutch oven or heavy, deep pot add the pinto and black beans and water; bring to a boil and cook for 15 minutes. Add remaining ingredients. Reduce to a simmer, cover with a tight lid, and cook for2 ½ hours.

Every half hour, stir beans and check water level. Add extra water as needed. Sauce should be slightly thick and soupy.

Kathryn Swarthout is the author of six juvenile novels and was a columnist for *Woman's Day* for twenty years. She is the recipient of a Certificate of Merit in Literature from the National Society of Arts & Letters. She co-authored several books with her late husband, Glendon Swarthout, including *Whichaway*. She is currently updating this novel for today's young readers.

Glendon Swarthout received two Spur awards and the Lifetime Achievement Award from Western Writers of America. Incidentally, every Western written by Glendon Swarthout was either optioned, sold, or finally produced into a film.

Their son, Miles Swarthout, is noted for his exceptional screenplays, including *The Shootist*.

WHICHAWAY

Nobody said much at chuck. They ate. This particular morning the boy put away three eggs sunny-side-up, a hill of fried potatoes, five sourdough biscuits with sorghum on them, and two cuts of leftover dried-apple pie. To irrigate this breakfast he used a cup of black coffee powerful enough to poison rats.

Published by Northland Publishing

A Hill of Fried Potatoes

RECIPE COURTESY OF KATHRYN SWARTHOUT

The best way to prepare this dish is on a griddle. If you don't have a griddle, use a large skillet, preferably a cast-iron one.

> 3 tablespoons butter
> 1 cup (1 large) chopped onion
> ½ cup (1 medium) chopped green bell pepper
> 4 cups (1- to 1¼-pound) potatoes, cooked and cut in ½-inch cubes
> 2 cups (½- to ¾-pound) beef steak cut in ¼-inch cubes
> ½ teaspoon each salt and black pepper
> ¼ cup evaporated milk (regular milk will do)
> healthy squirt Tabasco or other hot pepper sauce (optional)

Heat griddle until a drop of water quickly sizzles away. Add the butter, melt it, and coat the griddle. Add onions and bell pepper; sauté.

Add potatoes, beef cubes, and salt and pepper. Fry for 3 minutes, turning once.

Sprinkle the milk and Tabasco over all and stir to mix. Cook for 2 minutes, or until potatoes are golden brown on the bottom. Turn and brown the other side.

Serve in a heap on a warmed plate.

L on Walters wrote articles for the *San Diego Union* before moving to Arizona. Now he pens a column titled "Food for Thought" for the *Sedona Red Rock News*. In addition, he writes articles on horses and the baking techniques of the Old West. He is the author of *The Old West Baking Book* (Northland Publishing). Walters lives in Sedona, Arizona.

EXCERPT FROM

THE OLD WEST BAKING BOOK

Although the Pennsylvania Dutch have laid claim to this popular dessert, it was often fixed on the open range as a breakfast dish. Sometimes called a molasses cake, its popularity was understandable. Ingredients were on hand, assembly was easy, and varieties abounded. The chuck wagon cook could be the day's hero by quickly throwing together basic goods and serving it piping hot, either as a pie or smaller pastry.

There are two schools of thought on preparation. The East Coast version used huge amounts of butter. With few dairy products available on the open range, cooks of the West preferred lard. There is a simple compromise—olid vegetable shortening. It keeps the crust from getting soggy and cuts down on cholesterol.

Published by Northland Publishing

Southwest Shoofly Pie

RECIPE COURTESY OF LON WALTERS

2 cups all-purpose flour
½ cup granulated sugar
½ cup solid shortening

1 cup light molasses
1 teaspoon baking soda
1 cup boiling water

Preheat oven to 375°F.

Combine flour, sugar, and shortening. Blend with a pastry knife, or quickly in a food processor, until crumbly like oatmeal.

Place the crumbly mixture in a greased pie pan, and spread evenly on the bottom and up the sides, being careful not to compress the mix.

Blend molasses, baking soda, and boiling water; carefully pour over the crumbs. Bake for 45 minutes. Sides will be slightly puffy when done.

Cool before serving and slice like a pie.

If the pie breaks apart, or you desire variety, scoop it out and serve in a dish topped with whipped cream. No one will ever know the difference.

Sandy Whiting is best known for her short fiction. Among these is "Charity," published by *Louis L'Amour Western Magazine*. "Charity" was the 1994 Western Writers of America Spur winner for best short fiction. Whiting resides in Wichita, Kansas.

EXCERPT FROM

CHARITY

From the berry patch, I could see a summer squall brewing to the northwest. I figured I had about an hour left before it came calling. I picked faster and faster, never minding if I didn't get all the green caps off. I could do that later. My mouth watered with the thought of fresh strawberry pie.

My two buckets full, I was fixin' to leave when lightning struck a nearby tree. I was so close to it, I felt the electricity bounce off the tree and into me. Stunned, I stepped backwards, right into a prairie dog hole.

Published by Louis L'Amour Western Magazine

Fresh Strawberry Pie

RECIPE COURTESY OF SANDY WHITING

1 cup all-purpose flour
½ cup butter
1½ ounces cream cheese
½ cup powdered sugar

8 ounces whipped dairy topping
4 cups sliced strawberries
4 teaspoons granulated sugar

Preheat oven to 350°F.

Combine flour and butter to make a stiff dough. Pat into a pie pan and form a pie crust. Bake for 25 minutes or until lightly browned. Cool.

Combine cream cheese, powdered sugar, and 2 ounces of the whipped topping. Beat until smooth, then spread over bottom of cooled crust and up the sides.

Coat the strawberries with the granulated sugar. Carefully spoon the strawberry mix on top of the cream cheese mixture. Top with dollops of remaining whipped topping.

Refrigerate until ready to serve.

Jeanne Williams has written several acclaimed historical novels including *New York Times* best-seller *The Cave Dreamers*, the classic *A Lady Bought With Rifles,* and *Home Station.* Williams has won four WWA Spur Awards and the Levi Strauss Award for lifetime achievement in Western literature. One of her recent books is *The Unplowed Sky.* Williams lives in Portal, Arizona.

EXCERPT FROM

THE UNPLOWED SKY

Sophie climbed into the flivver, displaying plenty of shapely leg, and drove off as fast as she could. "Sure hope Garth stays clear of her," Shaft declared. "That's one mean female in spite of her soft look. Well, we better get to it, Hallie."

She peeled a dishpan of potatoes, strung and snapped a big kettle of green beans and baked three pineapple pies with juice oozing through the latticed crusts to turn golden brown. After Shaft took his luscious-smelling burnt-sugar cake out of the oven, she produced a heap of oat-meal cookies for morning lunch and mopped the floor.

Shaft tended two big skillets of frying chicken while Hallie chopped two cabbages into slaw and made biscuits and mashed potatoes. As if the success of the meal depended on him, Jackie held up fingers as he counted out plates, cups, and utensils and set the table. Hallie had scarcely filled the washbasins and put out clean towels when the whistle sounded.

It was 6:30, only about three hours since the men had demolished a big lunch, but they devoured chicken, biscuits, and mounds of vegetables as if they hadn't eaten in weeks. Conversation was limited to a terse "Please pass the smashed taters," or "Shoot the biscuits this way, will you?" It was only with chunks of pie, hunks of cake, and second or third or fourth cups of coffee that the men relaxed.

Published by St. Martin's Press, Inc.

Shaft's Burnt Sugar Cake

RECIPE COURTESY OF JEANNE WILLIAMS

1½ cups plus 2 tablespoons sugar	*1 teaspoon vanilla extract*
½ cup butter	*2½ cups all-purpose flour*
2 egg yolks, whites reserved	*1 cup milk*
2 tablespoons water	*2 teaspoons baking powder*

Preheat oven to 350°F.

In a large bowl, combine 1½ cups sugar and butter and blend until creamy. Add egg yolks and mix well.

Place 2 tablespoons sugar in a heavy skillet. Stir constantly over high heat until it is melted, brown, and begins to smoke. Keep sugar scraped from sides of skillet. Boil water and add twoo tablespoons to sugar: stir.

Add egg mixture and vanilla extract, and mix well. Add two cups of flour and milk by turns, beating thoroughly between each addition.

In a mixing bowl, combine baking powder with ½ cup of the flour. In a separate bowl beat egg whites into peaks and fold into flour mixture, then add to cake mix. Blend well.

Bake 1 hour.

Cool. Use frosting of choice.

Bob Wiseman is the author of *Healthy Southwestern Cooking* (Northland Publishing). His freelance historical, rodeo and cowboy, outdoor, and Western-cuisine articles have appeared in various media such as *American Cowboy Magazine, Wild West Magazine, Chile Pepper Magazine, Rocky Mountain Game and Fish,* and *Las Vegas Review Journal.* In addition, he's a frequent contributor to *The Tombstone Epitaph.* Wiseman lives part-time on the road near a trout stream or, most of the time, in Las Vegas, Nevada.

EXCERPT FROM

CROSSING THE FLAVOR FRONTIER

Long before the Battle of the Alamo, before a border divided Mexico and the United States, there was another border, an invisible border.

This imprecise boundary line . . . wasn't determined by rivers, barbed wire, mountain ranges or section markers. Instead, the trail was defined by aromas—the wonderful smell of chiles roasting, frijoles with onions and garlic simmering in a clay pot, tortillas toasting and all the other marvelous flavors that make up the now-celebrated tastes of the Southwest. The border was an aromatic belt of flavorful food.

Some call this style of cooking Tex-Mex or Sonoran or Mexican or *too darned spicy for me, Bob.* I call it Southwestern cooking or Border Vittles, because that's what it is—a culinary blend of cultures.

Published by American Cowboy Magazine

Black Bean Frijoles

RECIPE COURTESY OF BOB WISEMAN

> 1 tablespoon canola oil
> ½ cup (1 breast) chicken, cooked and diced
> ½ cup onion, chopped
> 2 cloves garlic, minced
> 1 pound dried black beans, sorted and washed
> 3 cups chicken stock
> 1 cup water
> 1 teaspoon fresh oregano (or ¼ tsp. dried)
> ½ teaspoon salsa habañero (or other hot Mexican-style sauce)
> ¼ teaspoon salt

Heat a deep skillet or Dutch oven until a drop of water quickly sizzles away. Add canola oil and chicken and sauté until chicken becomes light brown. Add onion and garlic and sauté until onion is limp. Add black beans, chicken broth, and 1 cup water. Bring to a low boil and add oregano, salsa habanero and salt. Boil for 5 minutes.

Reduce to a simmer. Cover and continue to simmer for 2 to 2½ hours, or until beans are soft. Add extra water as needed.

Remove from heat and let cool. Puree half of the frijoles in a blender, then combine with the original mixture.

Re-heat to desired consistency (the longer you cook it, the thicker it gets). If you like, serve with shredded cheese on top.

Sally Zanjani, for the most part, writes nonfiction. Her titles include *Goldfield: The Last Gold Rush on the Western Frontier* (Swallow Press/Ohio University Press), *Jack Longstreet: Last of the Desert Frontiersmen* (University of Nevada Press), and *Ghost Dance Winter and Other Tales of the Frontier* (Nevada Historical Society), winner of the Westerners International Award. Zanjani also has written over forty magazine articles for *Nevada, American West, and Montana: Magazine of Western History*. Her latest book is *A Mine of Her Own: Women Prospectors in the American West 1850–1950* (University of Nebraska Press). Zanjani lives at the foot of the Sierra Nevadas in Reno, Nevada.

EXCERPT FROM

GOLDFIELD: THE LAST GOLD RUSH ON THE WESTERN FRONTIER

Goldfield remained within the traditions of the mining camp gourmand. Even the delicatessens featured offerings likely to appeal to the most discriminating palate—stuffed mangoes, for example. Oysters, long prized as the ultimate dining luxury despite the logistical difficulties of transportation across the deserts before spoilage set in, often appeared on the sumptuous sounding restaurant menus. . . . Those who took the special seventy-five cent breakfast at the Goldfield Hotel grill were offered not only the usual hotcakes, biscuits, eggs, fried mush, and citrus fruits, but also strawberries or raspberries in cream, boiled salt mackerel, steak, mutton, pork chops, and fried calves liver.

Aside from Victor Ajax's La Parisienne, the most renowned restaurant in the city was probably the Palm Grill, a two-story affair able to accommodate two hundred guests in private dining rooms and elegantly appointed main dining halls on both levels. Carl Glasscock later recalled the strange juxtoposition between this refined restaurant and the crudites of journeying to Goldfield on a stormy night in an open stage while large numbers of coyotes prowled and howled on the outskirts of the city: half an hour later we were in the Palm Grill, washed and warmed, with Julius Goldsmith's violin displacing the mournful howls of the coyotes, and quail on toast before us on fine china laid upon immaculate linen.

Published by Swallow Press/Ohio University Press

Goldfield Hotcakes for Two

RECIPE BY SALLY ZANJANI

½ cup pancake mix
⅓ cup cornmeal
⅓ cup rolled oats
½ teaspoon salt

1 egg, whipped
1½ cup buttermilk
vegetable oil for grilling

In a deep bowl combine all the above ingredients, except the vegetable oil. Apply a thin coat of vegetable oil to a griddle or a wide skillet. Pour several dollops of the batter onto the griddle, keeping them about a half inch apart.

Turn the pancakes when they start to bubble and the edges seem dry.

Remove the pancakes when the bottom is golden brown and stack on a warmed plate.

Repeat the process until all the batter is used.

Serve with butter, and maple syrup, honey, fruit preservatives, or raspberries and cream; accompany with T-bone steak, or pork chops and eggs.

Norm Zollinger is one of the best-loved authors of fiction set in the American Southwest. Zollinger won the Golden Spur Award in 1979 for his first novel, *Riders to Cibola,* which remained on the *Albuquerque Journal* best-seller list for ninetynine weeks (seventeen weeks at the number one position). In 1981 Zollinger published a second western epic, *Corey Lane,* a fictional account of the Victorio War in New Mexico. *Corey Lane* spent nineteen weeks at number one on the *Journal* list. Since then Zollinger has written several more books, including *Chapultepec, Not of War Only, Lautrec, Rage in Chupadera,* and *Passage to Quivira.*

⇒•⇐

EXCERPT FROM

PASSAGE TO QUIVIRA

He laughed.

"What's so funny?" Sam said.

"You've enough food here to last a week."

"Have we got a week?" She looked out across the lake. "God, but it's beautiful up here, Ian. Wish we had a year." There was a dream tone to her voice. . . .

She laid the meal out on the blanket. It wasn't what he would have called hearty food, but there was so much in the way of canapes, tiny trimmed sandwiches, two different pates, and even caviar and lemon wedges, that he knew the two of them couldn't eat it all. There were thin-stemmed glasses for his iced tea and for the half bottle of Pouilly-Fuisse she had brought along for herself.

They didn't talk as they ate, but he watched her closely, followed every mouthful of food she took. She wasn't a dainty eater. He had noticed that before. Samantha Edwards was a woman of highly developed senses in every way.

Published by Tor/Forge

⇒•⇐

Sandwich from the Lake of the Little Shadows

RECIPE COURTESY OF NORM ZOLLINGER

½ cup cream cheese
1 scallion, finely minced
pinch ground cumin
pinch garlic powder
pinch chili powder
pinch salt
pinch pepper
1 teaspoon lime juice
8 whole green chiles, washed, seeded, and halved
8 whole canned pimiento chiles, halved
8 slices pumpernickel bread, sliced thin

Blend in a glass or ceramic bowl the cream cheese, scallion, cumin, garlic, chili, powder, salt, pepper, and lime juice.

Lay out 4 slices of the pumpernickel. Cover completely with green chiles.

Gently layer the cream cheese over the chiles. Cover the cream cheese with pimientos.

With a very sharp knife, quarter the sandwiches in triangles or squares. Trim sides of sandwiches to eliminate excess chiles and cream cheese.

Sandwich from the Lake of the Little Shadows

Acknowledgments

Adare, Sierra. *Backcountry Cooking: Feasts for Hikers, Hoofers, and Floaters.* Boise, ID: Tamarack Books, Inc., 1996.

Alter, Judy. *Cherokee Rose.* New York: Bantam Doubleday Dell Publishing Group, Inc.

Arnold, Sam. *The Fort Restaurant: New Foods of the Old West.* New York: HarperCollins Publishers, 1997.

Bean, Fred. *Trails End.* New York: Zebra Books, 1994.

Birchfield, D.L. "Never Again." In *Blue Dawn, Red Earth: New Native American Storytellers,* edited by Cliff E. Trafzer, 298-299. New York: Anchor Books, 1996.

Blakely, Mike. *Shortgrass Song.* New York: Forge Books, 1994.

Bonner, Cindy. *Looking After Lily.* Chapel Hill, NC: Algonquin of Chapel Hill, 1994.

Braun, Matt. *The Savage Land.* New York: Popular Library, 1981.

Brown, Irene Bennett. *The Plainswoman.* New York: Ballantine Books, 1994.

Brown, Larry. *Hog Ranches of Wyomng: Liquor Lust & Lies Under Sagebrush Skies.* Glendo, WY: High Plains Press, 1995.

Browning, Sinclair. *Enju: the Life and Struggle of an Apache Chief from the Little Running Water.* Flagstaff, AZ: Northland Press, 1981.

Butrille, Susan G. *Women's Voices from the Oregon Trail.* Boise, ID: Tamarack Books, Inc., 1995.

Cano, Tony, and Anne Sochat. *Dutch Oven Cooking With Tony Cano.* Scottsdale, AZ: Reata Publishing Co., 1993.

Carlson, Laurie. *Westward Ho!* Chicago: Chicago Review Press, Inc., 1996.

Carroll, Murray. "The Peripatetic Oyster." In *True West,* July, 1992.

Clayton, Paul. *Calling Crow.* New York: Berkley Publishing Group, 1995.

Cleary, Rita. *Goldtown.* Santa Fe, NM: Sunstone Press, 1996.

Cobb, Colin P. *Cowboy Cookin'.* Organ, NM: WordWright Press, 1992.

Coldsmith, Don. *Daughter of the Eagle.* New York: Bantam Doubleday Dell Publishing Group, Inc., 1998.

Crutchfield, James A. *Eyewitness to History.* Boise, ID: Tamarack Books, Inc, 1996.

Cunningham, Chet. *Survival Trail.* London: Robert Hale Ltd., 1995

Cunningham, Sharon. *Dixie Gun Works' Book of Southern Recipes.* Union City, TN: Pioneer Press, 1994.

Curtis, Jack. *The Quiet Cowboy.* New York: Pocket Books, 1994.

Dequasie, Andrew. *Thirsty.* New York: Walker & Co., 1983.

Duncklee, John. "View From the Porch." *The Connection ,* Arivaca, AZ.

Estleman, Loren D. *City of Widows.* New York: Forge, 1996.

Etter, Jim Marion. *Ghost-town Tales of Oklahoma: Unforgettable Stories of Nearly*

Forgotten Places. Stillwater, OK: New Forums Press, Inc., 1996.

Fackler, Elizabeth. *Billy the Kid: the Legend of El Chivato.* New York: Forge/St. Martin's Press, Inc., 1995.

de la Garza, Phyllis. *Chaco.* Syracuse, NY: New Readers Press, publishing division of Laubach Literacy International, 1990.

Gear, Kathleen O'Neal. *Thin Moon and Cold Mist.* New York: Forge, 1995.

Gear, Michael W. *Long Ride Home.* New York: Forge, 1995.

Gibson, Robin. *The Doctor of Whiskey City.* New York: Avalon, 1995.

Hackenberry, Charles. *I Rode With Jesse James.* HarperCollins, 1996.

Hughes, Stella. *Chuck Wagon Cookin'.* Tucson, AZ: University of Arizona Press, 1974.

Ihle, Sharon. *The Bride Wore Spurs.* New York: Harper Paperbacks, 1995.

Jakes, John. *California Gold.* New York: Ballantine Books, 1990.

Jameson, W.C. "A Man Must Have his Meat." In *Log Cabin Democrat.*

Kimmel, Fred N. *Song of the Plains.* New York: Macmillan Publishing USA, 1963.

Knight, Arthur Winfield. *The Secret Life of Jesse James.* Lenoir, NC: BurnhillWolf, 1996.

Lanza, Ruth Willet. "The Last Encounter." In *Raconteur,* April, 1996.

Legg, John. *Guns of Arizona.* New York: Zebra Books, 1992.

Leonard, Elmore. *Gunsights.* New York: Bantam Books, 1979.

Lewis, Preston. *The Lady and Doc Holliday.* Austin, TX: Diamond Books, 1989.

Linck, Ernestine Sewell. *Eats: a Folk History of Texas Foods.* Fort Worth, TX: Texas Christian University Press, 1989.

Long, Elaine. *Bittersweet Country.* New York: St. Martin's Press, Inc., 1991.

Lynde, Stan. *The Bodacious Kid.* Kalispell, MT: Cottonwood Publications, 1996.

Martin, Kat. *Midnight Rider.* New York: St. Martin's Press, Inc., 1996.

Martin, Larry J. *The Benicia Belle.* New York: Bantam Books, 1993.

Megeath, Joe. "The Wooly West." In *Wild West Magazine.* 1997.

Moulton, Candy. *Roadside History of Wyoming.* Missoula, MT: Mountain Press Publishing Co., 1995.

Nixon, Joan Lowery. *In the Face of Danger: an Orphan Train Adventure.* New York: Bantam Doubleday Dell Publishing Group, Inc., 1988.

Palmer, James. *Game Wardens vs. Poachers: Tickets Still Available.* Iola, WI: Krause Publications, 1993

Pepper, Choral. *Treasure Legends of the West.* Layton, UT: Gibbs Smith Publisher, 1994.

Petersen, Gwen. *Cow Camp Cookery.* Big Tree, MT: Sow's Ear Press,

Post, George. *Out of the Fast Lane.* Pittsburgh, PA: Dorrance Publishing, 1993.

Recknor, Ellen. *Me and the Boys.* New York: Berkley Publishing Group, 1995.

Roach, Joyce Gibson. "A Two Gun Man." In *New Trails: Twenty-Three Original*

Stories of the West from Western Writers of America, edited by Martin H. Greenberg and John Jakes. New York: Bantam Books, 1995.

Roberts, Mark K. *Gallows Rider.* New York: Zebra Books, 1986.

Roe, JoAnn. *The North Cascadians.* Seattle: Madrona Publishers, 1980.

Sherlock, Patti. *Four of a Kind.* New York: Holiday House, 1991.

Shockley, W.M. "Bustout." In *Louis L'Amour Western Magazine,* January, 1995.

Slatta, Richard. *The Cowboy Encyclopedia.* Santa Barbara, CA: ABC-CLIO, 1994.

Swarthout, Glendon and Kathryn Swarthout. *Whichaway.* Revised edition by Kathryn Swarthout. Flagstaff, AZ: Northland Publishing, 1997.

Walters, Lon. *The Old West Baking Book.* Flagstaff, AZ: Northland Publishing, 1996.

Whiting, Sandy. "Charity." In *Louis L'Amour Western Magazine,* January, 1995.

Williams, Jeanne. *The Unplowed Sky.* New York: St. Martin's Press, Inc., 1994.

Wiseman, Bob. "Crossing the Flavor Frontier." In *American Cowboy Magazine,* March/April, 1995.

Zanjani, Sally. *Goldfield: the Last Gold Rush on the Western Frontier.* Athens, OH: Swallow Press/Ohio University Press, 1992.

Zollinger, Norm. *Passage to Quivira.* New York: Tor/Forge Books, 1996.

Index

Adare, Sierra, 2–3
Alter, Judy, 4–5
Apple Butter, 102
Apple Compote, 82
Apples, 82, 102, 116
Arnold, Sam, 6–8

Backcountry Cooking, 2
Bacon
    Green Beans with Pecan Sauce and Bacon,
        89, 90
Baked Beans, 23
Bananas, 116
Barbecued Guaymas Red Snapper, 82
Bean, Fred, 9
Beans
    Black Bean Frijoles, 128–129
    Bunkhouse Beans, 122
    Cave Man Beans, 61
    Celsa's Chile Beans, 53
    Prohibition Bean Dip, 117
    Sunday Baked Beans, 23
Beef
    Guisado Monterey (Monterey-Style
        Stew), 93
    A Hill of Fried Potatoes, 123
    Jerky—Pingora Style, 3
    One-Pot Chop Suey, 109
    Running Eagle's Beef Jerky, 37
    Son-of-a-Bitch Stew, 16
    Texas Brisket, 73
Benecia Belle, 94
Billy the Kid: The Legend of El Chivato, 52
Birchfield, D. L., 10–11
Biscuits
    Lynda's Baking Powder Biscuits, 92
Bittersweet Country, 88
Black Bean Frijoles, 128–129
Black Walnut and Ginger Shrimp Stir Fry, 119
Blakely, Mike, 12–13
Bocadillos Mejicanos (Mexican appetizers),
    115, 116
The Bodacious Kid, 91
Bonner, Cindy, 14–15
The Bowl of the Wife of Kit Carson, 6, *7,* 8
Braun, Matt, 15–16
Breads and baked goods. *See also* Cakes, Pancakes,
    Pies and cobblers
    Candy's Spudnuts, 99
    Frybread, 35
    Lynda's Baking Powder Biscuits, 92
    Mom McBain's Light Bread, 5
    Tortilla Soup, 49

Two-Skillet Campfire Cornbread, 11
The Bride Wore Spurs, 66
Brown, Irene Bennett, 17
Brown, Larry, 19–20
Browning, Sinclair, 22
Buffalo Hump, 60
Bunkhouse Beans, 122
Burnt Sugar Cake, 127
Bust Out, 120
Butruille, Susan, 23

Cakes
    Old-Fashioned Pound Cake, 87
    Shaft's Burnt Sugar Cake, 127
Caldo Tlapeno, 6, 8
California Gold, 69
Calling Crow, 30
Camarones Borrachos (Drunken Shrimp), 47
Candy's Spudnuts, 99
Cano, Tony, 24–25
Canteloupe, 116
Carlson, Laurie, 26
Carne de Puerco (Shredded Pork), 31
Carroll, Murray, 27–29
Carson, Kit, 6, 8
Cave Man Beans, 61
Celsa's Chile Beans, 53
Chaco, 54
Charity, 125
Cherokee Rose, 4
Chicken
    The Bowl of the Wife of Kit Carson, *7,* 8
    Pot Pie, 13
    Spicy Barbecue Drumsticks, 25
Chicken Pot Pie, 13
Chokecherry Jelly, 33
Chop Suey, 109
Chuck Wagon Cookin', 64
"Chuckwagon Charley", 24
City of Widows, 48
Clayton, Paul, 30–31
Cleary, Rita, 32–33
Cobb, Colin, 34–35
Cobblers. *See* Pies and cobblers
Coldsmith, Don, 36–37
Corn
    bread, 11, 104–105
    Popcorn Balls, 26
    Pioneer Corn Pudding, 17, *18*
Cornbread
    Pepper's Dutch-Oven Cornbread Casserole,
        104–105
    Two-Skillet Campfire Cornbread, 11

Cow Camp Cookery, 106
Cowboy Cookin', 34
The Cowboy Encyclopedia, 121
Crossing the Flavor Frontier, 128
Crutchfield, James A., 38–39
Cunningham, Chet, 40–41
Cunningham, Sharon, 42–43

Daughter of the Eagle, 36
de la Garza, Phyllis. See Garza, Phyllis de la
"Dee-zerts," 64
Deep-Fried Rattler, 41
Dequasie, Andrew, 44–45
Desserts. See also Cakes; Jelly, etc.; Pies and
        cobblers
    Apple Compote, 82
    "Dee-zerts," 64
    Homemade Butterscotch Ice Cream, 78
    Pioneer Corn Pudding, 17, 18
    Popcorn Balls, 26
Dixie Gun Works' Best of Southern Recipes, 42
The Doctor of Whiskey City, 61
Donegal Pie, 67, 68
Doughnuts
    Candy's Spudnuts, 99
Drumsticks, 25
Duck
    Lou's Duck & Wild Rice, 43
Duncklee, John, 46–47
Dutch Oven Cooking with Tony Cano, 24

Eats: A Folk History of Texas Foods, 86–87
Egg Gravy, 15
Elk Steaks, 20, 21
Emma's Chokecherry Jelly, 33
Enju: The Life and Struggle of an Apache Chief
        from the Little Running Water, 22
Estleman, Loren D., 48–49
Etter, Jim Marion, 50–51
Eyewitness to American History, 38

Fackler, Elizabeth, 52–53
Faux Venison, 45
The Fort Restaurant: New Foods of the Old West, 6
Four of a Kind, 118
Fresh Strawberry Pie, 126
Frybread, 35

Gallows Riders, 114
Game Wardens vs. Poachers: Tickets Still Available,
        102–103
Gamma Lewis's Pecan Pie, 85, 86
Garza, Phyllis de la, 54–56
Gear, Kathleen O'Neal, 57–59
Gear, W. Michael, 58–60
Ghost-Town Tale of Oklahoma, 50
Gibson, Robin, 61
Golden Spur awards. See Spur awards
Goldfield: The Last Gold Rush on the Western
        Frontier, 129–130

Goldfield Hotcakes for Two, 130
Goldtown, 32
Gravy, 15
Green Beans with Pecan Sauce and Bacon, 89, 90
Griddled Elk Steaks, 20, 21
Guisado Monterey (Monterey-Style Stew), 93
Guns of Arizona, 81
Gunsights, 82–83

Hackenberry, Charles, 62–63
Hangtown Fry, 28, 29
A Hill of Fried Potatoes, 123
Hog Ranches of Wyoming: Liquor, Lust & Lies
        Under Sagebrush Skies, 19
Homemade Butterscotch Ice Cream, 78
Hughes, Stella, 64–65

I Rode with Jesse James, 62
Ice cream
        Homemade Butterscotch Ice Cream, 78
Ihle, Sharon, 66–68
In the Face of Danger, 100

Jakes, John, 69–71
Jameson, W. C., 72–73
Jelly, etc.
        Apple Butter, 102
        Emma's Chokecherry Jelly, 33
Jerky
        Jerky—Pingora Style, 3
        Running Eagle's Beef Jerky, 37
Jicama, 116

Kate's Donegal Pie, 67, 68
Kimmel, Fred N., 74–75
Knight, Arthur Winfield, 76–78

The Lady and Doc Holliday, 84
Lamb
        Savory Leg of Lamb, 97
        Shimázan's Lamb Stew, 80
Lamb Stew, 80
Lanza, Ruth Willett, 79–80
The Last Encounter, 79
Legg, John, 81–82
Leonard, Elmore, 82–83
Lewis, Preston, 84–86
Linck, Ernestine Sewell, 86–87
Long, Elaine, 88–90
Long Ride Home, 58–60
Looking After Lily, 14
Lou's Duck & Wild Rice, 43
Lynda's Baking Powder Biscuits, 92
Lynde, Stan, 91–92

Machaca, 31
A Man Must Have His Meat, 72
Martin, Kat, 92–93
Martin, Larry J., 94–95
Me and the Boys, 110

Meat. *See also* Jerky, Poultry
    Carne de Puerco (Shredded Pork), 31
    Deep-Fried Rattler, 41
    Faux Venison, 45
    Griddled Elk Steaks, 20, *21*
    Guisado Monterey (Monterey-Style
      Stew), 93
    A Man Must Have His Meat, 72
    Pan-Fried Squirrel, 120–121
    Pozole and Pork Chops, 95
    Roast Buffalo Hump, 60
    Savory Leg of Lamb, 97
    Shimázan's Lamb Stew, 80
    Son-of-a-Bitch Stew, 16
    Texas Brisket, 73
    Venison Roast, 75
Medicine Pipe Bearer's Award, 1
Megeath, Joe, 96–97
Midnight Rider, 93
Milk Pie, 63
Mom McBain's Light Bread, 5
Moulton, Candy, 98–99
My Pecan Pie, 110–111

Never Again, 10
Nine-Raisin Rice, 103
Nixon, Joan Lowery, 100–102
The North Cascadians, 117
Nuts
    Black Walnut and Ginger Shrimp Stir
      Fry, 119
    Gamma Lewis's Pecan Pie, *85,* 86
    Green Beans with Pecan Sauce and Bacon,
      89, 90
    My Pecan Pie, 110–111
Nye, Nelson C. "Nels," 1

Oklahoma-Style Fried Okra, 51
Okra, 51
Old-Fashioned Peach Cobbler, 9
Old-Fashioned Pound Cake, 87
The Old West Baking Book, 124
One-Pot Chop Suey, 109
Out of the Fast Lane, 108
Owen Wister Award, 1
Oysters
    Hangtown Fry, 28, *29*

Palmer, Jim, 102–103
Pan-Fried Squirrel, 120–121
Pancakes
    Goldfield Hotcakes for Two, 130
    Sourdough Starter & Sourdough Pancakes,
      107–108
Papayas, 116
Passage to Quivira, 131
Peach Cobbler, 9, 113
Peanut Soup, 39

Pecan Pie, *85,* 86, 110–111
Pecans
    Gamma Lewis's Pecan Pie, *85,* 86
    Green Beans with Pecan Sauce and Bacon,
      89, 90
    My Pecan Pie, 110–111
Pepper, Choral, 104–105
Pepper's Dutch-Oven Cornbread Casserole,
    104–105
The Peripatetic Oyster, 27
Petersen, Gwen, 106–108
Pies and cobblers
    Chicken Pot Pie, 13
    Fresh Strawberry Pie, 126
    Gamma Lewis's Pecan Pie, *85,* 86
    Kate's Donegal Pie, *67, 68*
    Milk Pie, 63
    My Pecan Pie, 110–111
    Old-Fashioned Peach Cobbler, 9
    Ranch-Style Peach Cobbler, 113
    Southwest Shoofly Pie, 125
    Vinegar Cobbler, 65
    Wild Rice Pie, 58, *59*
Pioneer Corn Pudding, 17, *18*
The Plainswoman, 17
Popcorn Balls, 26
Pork
    Carne de Puerco (Shredded Pork), 31
    Pozole and Pork Chops, 95
Post, George, 108–109
Pot Pie, 13
Potatoes
    A Hill of Fried Potatoes, 123
Poultry
    Chicken Pot Pie, 13
    Lou's Duck & Wild Rice, 43
    Spicy Barbecue Drumsticks, 25
    Stuffed Roasted Cornish Game Hen, 70, *71*
Pozole
    Pozole and Pork Chops, 95
    Snake Killer's Pozole, 22
Pozole and Pork Chops, 95
Prickly Pear Leaves (Stuffed), *55, 56*
Prohibition Bean Dip, 117
Pudding, 17, *18*

Rabbit
    Faux Venison, 45
Ranch-Style Peach Cobbler, 113
Rattler, 41
Recknor, Ellen, 110–111
Red Snapper, 82
Roach, Joyce Gibson, 112–113
Roadside History of Wyoming, 98
Roast Buffalo Hump, 60
Roberts, Mark, 114–116
Roe, JoAnn, 117
Roundup, 1

Running Eagle's Beef Jerky, 37

Sandwich from the Lake of the Little Shadows,
    132, *133*
The Savage Land, 15
Savory Leg of Lamb, 97
Seafood
    Barbecued Guaymas Red Snapper, 82
    Black Walnut and Ginger Shrimp Stir
        Fry, 119
    Camarones Borrachos (Drunken Shrimp),
        47
    Hangtown Fry (oysters), *28, 29*
The Secret Life of Jesse James, 76
Shaft's Burnt Sugar Cake, 127
Sherlock, Patti, 118–119
Shimázan's Lamb Stew, 80
Shockley, W. M., 120–121
Shoofly Pie, 125
Shortgrass Song, 12
Shrimp
    Black Walnut and Ginger Shrimp Stir
        Fry, 119
    Camarones Borrachos (Drunken
        Shrimp), 47
Slatta, Richard, 121–122
Snake Killer's Pozole, 22
Sochat, Ann, 24–25
Son-of-a-Bitch Stew, 16
Song of the Plains, 74
Soup
    The Bowl of the Wife of Kit Carson,
        6, 8
    Caldo Tlapeno, 6, *7,* 8
    Peanut Soup, 39
    Pozole, 22, 95
    Tortilla Soup, 49
Sourdough Starter & Sourdough Pancakes,
    107–108
Southwest Shoofly Pie, *85,* 125
Spicy Barbecue Drumsticks, 25
Spur awards, 1
Spur Banquet, 1
Squirrel
    Pan-Fried Squirrel, 120–121
Stew
    Guisado Monterey (Monterey-Style
        Stew), 93
    Lamb Stew, 80
    Son-of-a-Bitch (beef) Stew, 16
Stirrup Award, 1
Strawberry Pie, 126
Stuffed Prickly Pear Leaves, 56
Stuffed Roasted Cornish Game Hen, 70, *71*
Sunday Baked Beans, 23
Survival Trail, 40
Swarthout, Kathryn, 122–123

Texas Brisket, 73
Thin Moon and Cold Mist, 57

Thirsty, 44
Thompson, Thomas "Tommy," 1
Tortilla Soup, 49
Trails End, 8
Treasure Legends of the West, 104
A Two Gun Man, 112
Two-Skillet Campfire Cornbread, 11

The Unplowed Sky, 126–127

Vegetables
    Green Beans with Pecan Sauce and Bacon,
        89, 90
    Oklahoma-Style Fried Okra, 51
    One-Pot Chop Suey, 109
    Stuffed Prickly Pear Leaves, 56
Venison
    Faux Venison, 45
    Venison Roast, 75
The View from the Porch, 46–47
Vinegar Cobbler, 65

Walnuts
    Black Walnut and Ginger Shrimp Stir
        Fry, 119
Walters, Lon, 124–125
Western Writers of America, Inc., 1
Hall of Fame, 1
Westward Ho!, 26
Whichaway, 123
Whiting, Sandy, 125–126
Wild rice
    Lou's Duck & Wild Rice, 43
    Nine-Raisin Rice, 103
    Wild Rice Pie, 58, *59*
Williams, Jeanne, 126–127
Wiseman, Bob, 128–129
Wister Award. *See* Owen Wister Award
Women's Voices from the Oregon Trail, 23
The Wooly West, 96
WWA. *See* Western Writers of America, Inc.

Zanjani, Sally, 129–130
Zollinger, Norm, 131–133

Bob Wiseman has had a serious interest in the cooking of the greater Southwest since he moved to Las Vegas, Nevada, in 1954. In addition to publishing the popular *Healthy Southwestern Cooking* (Northland Publishing) and more than one hundred recipes in various journals, he has seen into print many pieces of short fiction and articles on Western history and Western outdoors. Wiseman is proud to be an active member of Western Writers of America.